WE AMERICANS

WE AMERICANS

A STUDY OF CLEAVAGE
IN AN AMERICAN CITY

BY

ELIN L. ANDERSON

NEW YORK / RUSSELL & RUSSELL

To

BURLINGTON

IN DEEP APPRECIATION OF WHAT IT IS
AND WHAT IT MAY BECOME

PREFACE

THE traditional pattern of American democracy is being revamped, not suddenly through forces of revolution but slowly and in response to natural events. Most Americans are not yet aware of the nature of these events; they know that something is happening to us and our culture but they are not able to give this "something" a proper name. Basic change *must* come slowly in this country. It can come rapidly only in those civilizations accustomed to authority and infused with a mystical conception of the state. Change comes rapidly with us only on the level of technology. Our culture, to use the famous phrase of Pericles, is a "happy diversity," and where there is diversity there is also resistance to patterned uniformity. Those who believe that a completely rationalized pattern of society might be imposed upon this nation quickly and suddenly labor under a misapprehension; they do not understand the deeply pluralistic character of American Society.

Pluralism in America is not a consciously-devised philosophy of life. On the contrary, it arises from the structures of our various governments, from the essential regionalism of a continental nation, and from the heterogeneity of our population. If we are to comprehend the nature of current alterations in our traditional democracy, we must examine more carefully each of the above features of our society. Our governmental structures, for example, were designed to prevent the rise of a strong centralized national government. But we have been moving in the direction of such a centralized government during a period of more than a half-century. This trend seems to me inevitable and proceeds at approximately the same rate regardless of which political party happens to be in power at Washington. If it proceeds far enough, the democratic process in this country will be obliged to operate under the dispensation of a bureaucracy. If, on the other hand, our democracy is to be saved from bureaucratic control, the corrective must come from an awakened regionalism. Regional pluralism is not enough, however, because upon examination one invariably discovers that wherever a region is sufficiently strong to withstand the inroads of bureaucracy this strength derives from a sense of quality, of tone, of value, created in the day-to-day relations of diversified people living in local communities.

The promise of American democracy is resident in the life of local communities. Technology and industry tend to destroy or weaken our primary groups; the community can exist only in terms of primary groups, for the sense of community is lost when human relationships become impersonal. It was this sense or feeling of community which gave character to Athens at the height of its democratic glory. How are we to achieve a similar sense of community in a society in which science, technology, and industry have come to be the chief sources of dynamics? This question appears to me to represent the core of contemporary statesmanship.

The initial answer to the query posed above is obvious; we must learn more about the character of life in local American communities. What is thus learned must be presented to the reading public and made available to students. In short, the study which follows in the pages of this volume constitutes an effective response to my query. Here is presented a "slice" of regionalism, a New England town sufficiently small to be viewed as a whole and yet epitomizing all that is complex in our diversified American culture. Here are to be seen class distinctions, ethnic-group conflicts, religious suspicions, and all the various differences which defy uniformity and confound the demagogue. The author's knowledge of the intricacies of community life has been achieved through approved methods of social investigation but her instruments have been deftly concealed. She writes with the ease of one who has acquired insights more true and more precious than mere knowledge. The total consequence is an essay which elicits hearty commendation from the professional writer of this preface and personal admiration from the author's former teacher.

EDUARD C. LINDEMAN

New York School of Social Work
July, 1937

ACKNOWLEDGMENT

IN A study such as this it is difficult to make acknowledgment to the many people whose ideas and personalities have in one way or another influenced its development; only a few can here be mentioned by name, but this does not mean that I am not indebted to many others. To Professor Henry F. Perkins, Director of the Eugenics Survey of Vermont, I am grateful for permission to undertake the study and for his patience and faith during the three years in which it developed from its original plan, suitable to a brief annual report of the Survey, into its present form. To the Vermont Emergency Relief Administration I am indebted for furnishing the assistance of six qualified fieldworkers whose knowledge of the community and whose identification each with a different ethnic group made possible the inclusion of cultural detail which might otherwise have been neglected. I am especially grateful to a small group of people whose assistance at various stages of the study helped me to recognize expanding possibilities in the material — to Professor Herman Feldman of Dartmouth College for constructive criticism and encouragement at critical periods throughout the study; to Professor Ellsworth Huntington of Yale University for reading the manuscript and making pertinent suggestions; to Professor Robert S. Lynd of Columbia University for criticisms which challenged me to attempt to reach a standard I had not thought of setting for myself; to Edward J. Fitzgerald for his valuable assistance in editing the manuscript and thrashing out details. Anne Rome Cohen, Secretary of the Eugenics Survey, has given loyal help in varied aspects of the study. Above all, I wish to express my gratitude to the many citizens of Burlington and others who have helped by giving time and interest in thinking through with me the issues before the community. Of these I wish to thank especially those who volunteered their services in the preliminary survey that forms the basis of this study, and those who have critically read the manuscript.

For the selection of material and the interpretations placed upon it responsibility is wholly mine. I only hope that Burlington will not feel that I have been unduly critical of a community which made me welcome and with which I am deeply identified. What is here presented is intended as a picture of a process rather than as a criticism of a particular city.

E. L. A.

CONTENTS

ILLUSTRATIONS

WE AMERICANS

CHAPTER I

INTRODUCTION

TODAY in America social chasms separating citizen from citizen are widening with startling rapidity. Under the pressure of economic insecurity and political instability, the distrust which the various groups that make up America feel for each other deepens daily. Ready to the hand of an able demagogue are the emotional tools by which a people can be divided, a population robbed of its integrity and its living force. In addition to the economic conflicts dividing class from class, racial and religious prejudices which have always been potent forces in American life are reasserting themselves. They form the basis for cleavage in their own right or influence the new cleavages which are appearing. Daily the newspapers give fresh evidence of the development of such prejudices. In the South a Negro is lynched; in California American laborers rise up and protest that the Chinese and the Japanese have "invaded" their fields of endeavor; in the Southwest, Mexicans are refused rooms at hotels reserved for the exclusive use of "whites," and in some theatres they have to sit in a special section. In New York the Friends of New Germany gather to express their approval of Hitler's anti-Semitic activity, while the Jews and their sympathizers decide to boycott the Germans. The high dream of creating an American people of all the elements that have been borne into the country on successive waves of immigration is far from realization.

Terroristic organizations play their part in this struggle. At various times such groups, fed upon antagonism, have sprung up in America. The "Know-Nothing" party of the 1850's, with its opposition to the immigrant, became in the Ku-Klux Klan movement more markedly flavored with a religious and racial prejudice. This movement had a brief resurgence into notoriety in 1923–24, but since then it has become less active, and its place has been taken by other organizations. These more modern groups are modeled in method and aim on the groups in Germany with the assistance of which Hitler came to power; many of them are openly dedicated to the terrorizing of Jews, Catholics, and Communists. Another indication of the sense of insecurity and distrust which the depression and the attendant economic ills has engendered in the American people is afforded by the numerous "patriotic" laws which have recently found their way onto the books of various states. The Teachers' Oath, laws prohibiting the teaching of certain subjects in schools, the compulsory saluting of the flag, all these argue a dangerous narrowing of the definition of "Americanism" which is at variance with the very principles on which America was founded. Such laws are the first attacks upon the democratic liberties which we have held dear. That we have, to a large extent, accepted them complacently points to the need we have to find some scapegoat to bear the burden of responsibility for our economic disorders. Struggling with the economic and political disruption which signalizes the end of one period in our history, we are yielding more and more to the temptation to find in the alien the root of all evil. We are even beginning to talk of that mythical figure, the "pure" American, a genetic concept even more anomalous than the "pure" Aryan.

Against the dangers inherent in such an attitude has long stood the pervasive belief of a large bloc of our population in the "great American dream." Such things as have happened in Europe cannot happen here, it is contended, because the basic hopes and aims of America differ from those of other countries: what Americans want is to live and let live in the common endeavor to get ahead, and as long as that aim predominates America will remain the land of opportunity for all; freedom will be a possession so universal that if any man just "gets the breaks," whether he be a Jew or a Catholic, an Italian or a good Old American, he will scale the heights; Americans would not tolerate anything that would upset and divide this freest culture in which men have sought to grow sturdily independent and prosperous.

Whether such a belief is justified or not, the fact that it is held by a large proportion of our population is a potent force in offsetting the tendency to division of the American people. Yet the belief rests uneasily. Some of the very persons who are most vociferous in its defense seek to bolster their own faith by joining such organizations as the Black Legion.

It is against the background of this contemporary uncertainty that the following study is laid. By considering the adjustment of several ethnic groups in a single community it seeks to ascertain the extent to which the peoples of America hold common ideals and are united by a sense of common destiny; it seeks to show the extent to which each group at the same time feels free to develop its own life; and finally, it seeks to ascertain the extent to which cleavages between ethnic groups serve to enhance or moderate those cleavages which economic insecurity and political disillusionment are producing in the America of today.

The terms used in this study need definition insofar as they are not of common usage or have been given arbitrary meanings in order to facilitate classification. Instead of the more common word "race," the term "ethnic group" is used wherever possible, to distinguish groups of common cultural heritage and character. For purposes of simplification, the Jews, because of the many characteristics which they have in common, are dealt with as an ethnic group, although they are much less this than they are a socio-religious one. Since the exact ethnic origin of many individuals was difficult to determine, it was decided that for this study a person's ethnic stock should be determined by the nationality of his parents; and when the parents were of different nationalities, by the nationality of the father, if foreign born, or, if the father was American born and the mother foreign, by the nationality of the mother. This last decision was made in order to distinguish people of such parentage from those of older American lineage. Individuals selected for the detailed interviews were almost all of "pure" stock as far back as known.

The term "Old American" was originally meant to apply only to those of the fourth generation or later in this country, but was extended to include those claiming long ancestry in this country on one side of the family even though one grandparent had come from Canada, England, Scotland, or some other country. These persons had usually become thoroughly incorporated into the Old American group. The term "English Canadian" is used to distinguish all the Canadians who are not of French extraction.

The meaning given to "first," "second," and "third generation" had to be decided in a similar manner. Thus, by "first generation" is meant all those who have been born in a foreign country but who have come to America to make it their home; "second generation" includes children of such parents born in this country; and "third generation" consequently embraces all those whose grandparents were the immigrants. The Italians, Syrians, and Greeks are almost all of the first generation; among the Germans and the Jews, on the other hand, there are many adults of the second as well as of the first generation, and a few even of the third. Among the French Canadians and the Irish, there are adult representatives of three generations in this country, and a few even of the fourth generation who remain identified with their nationality groups. Among the Irish, however, there are few of the first generation, since most of them have died and few newcomers have arrived to take their places, while the ranks of first-generation French Canadians, on the other hand, are continually being replenished by newcomers from across the border.

This study was made under the auspices of the Eugenics Survey of Vermont. At first glance a study essentially sociological may seem outside the province of such an organization. The eugenist is interested in the American problem of ethnic adjustment primarily in terms of the biological blending through intermarriage of the most desirable qualities of peoples. Yet because he finds that racial and religious prejudices frequently stand in the way of the realization of any ideal biological blending, his first task becomes the understanding and elimination of the environmental causes of such prejudice. Hence such a study as this, whatever sociological purpose it may serve, is an attempt at providing some groundwork upon which may be built a eugenic program of the future, based upon a full and uninhibited appreciation of the intelligence, special abilities, and social qualities of our diverse peoples.

CHAPTER II

THE CITY SELECTED

THE city selected for study is Burlington, Vermont. Situated on the shore of Lake Champlain, it is the largest city in the state, having a population of a little less than 25,000. It has several industries but is no longer an industrial center. With the decline of the importance of Lake Champlain as a waterway, and the westward expansion of the country, its industrial enterprises decreased; and with the rise in the use of the automobile it began to take on its present character as a commercial center, serving a wide rural area. Culturally, also, Burlington is the center of the state, containing the state university and many other educational institutions.

The city rises on a hill that slopes gently upward for a mile from the eastern shore of the Lake. For background it has the sweep of the Green Mountains; for foreground the Lake, and the ever-varied vista of the distant Adirondacks. At the foot of the hill are the wharves and warehouses, shabby tenement houses, and railroad tracks; halfway up is the business section — one main street running parallel to the Lake and headed by a fine old church; on the upper slope is a residential section of large, comfortable houses and spacious lawns; on the very summit is the University. From the top of the hill one can catch a glimpse of the Lake at its foot, through avenues whose interlocking elms form long aisles of Gothic arches. The

unusual beauty of the setting has led many to voice senti-
ments similar to those expressed by William Dean Howells
when, gazing upon the Bay of Naples, he remarked: "The
most beautiful view of the world except one — a Lake
Champlain sunset as seen from Burlington."

All of Burlington, however, is not as lovely as this central
area. There is the north end, thickly settled, where there
are few elm-arched avenues; where many houses are close
together and some are dark, unpainted boxes; where lawns
are narrow strips of grass and the children play in the
streets for lack of any more suitable playground. This
side of the city has its own business section, which is
frequented by the "other half" of Burlington only when it
seeks a bargain. Then there is the isolated colony around
the cotton mill in the south end of town, where uniform
company houses shelter a group of workers whose connection with the rest of Burlington is slight. There is also
a settlement "under the hill," on the far side of the slope
that reaches to Winooski, a mill town of 5,000 inhabitants
one mile from the center of Burlington. This area, too,
especially at its further end, has shabby, narrow houses.
These neighborhoods, however, are little known to those
who live their lives along the central slope of the hill.

The way of life of Burlington is representative of the
way still followed by an appreciable proportion of the
American people. It is a rural way of life as distinguished
from the urban way to be found in industrial centers. It
is stable rather than transitional, and its emphases are on
individual rather than collective solutions to its problems.

Yet the way of life of Vermont is to be distinguished from that of similar communities in, for example, the Middle West, for Vermont has behind it a much longer tradition; in its life today can still be felt that quality of individualism which led the Green Mountain state to remain independent for fourteen years after all the other states then existing had recognized the sovereignty of the national government. It still maintains its mistrust of outsiders and outside influence; recently, for example, a bill for a national highway to run through the center of the state was defeated, in part at least because of the fear that such a highway would bring in "foreign" influence. "Foreign," to Vermont, is New York, Washington, anything outside its own boundaries, anything removed from the careful check of its watchful eye.

In addition to the independence thus exemplified, Vermont is essentially conservative; its force in national life has been that of a check upon too rapid change. During the depression it did not reach the depths that other states in the nation did, nor has it ever known the heights of prosperity reached by many parts of the country. If another boom should come, Vermont will temperately enjoy good times. Knowing neither the unrest of the more turbulent industrial centers nor the bitter disillusionment of the rural areas of the West and South, it has felt secure in an established way of life in which the individual's relation to his small surrounding society is one of responsibility and participation, while his relation to the world outside is one of cautious watchfulness. Any marked social change is looked upon as a direct threat to the very security of this tested way of life. Hence, when in the national election of 1936 the entire country by the greatest vote in its history expressed its approval of the social philosophy and policies of President Franklin D. Roosevelt, Vermont with Maine stood alone in its dissenting vote. As one Vermonter commented, "When the rest of the country accepts a social revolution, Vermont will vote the Democratic ticket."

Although this capacity to resist outside change does make for a secure little world, it tends to produce certain weaknesses within the life of the state. Only when extreme pressure threatens the life of the whole do the various groups work together. Under ordinary conditions, an infinite variety of classes and cliques refuse to play ball with the other fellow, often for some minor or petty reason.

Burlington in many respects epitomizes this Vermont way of life; it is conservative, rural, individualistic; in all respects it is moderate. There is little extreme poverty and no great wealth; it is a city of comfortable homes and established routines. The businesses are small; the business men are generally satisfied, careful rather than excessively ambitious, competing not so much with the world outside as with each other for the trade which the surrounding rural areas supply. Even the students in Burlington's educational institutions are drawn largely from within the state.

Part of this conservatism of Burlington is due to its

H. R. Stevens

COLLEGE STREET, BURLINGTON

moderate size; it is too big to be a small town, too small to be a city. It has lost personal neighborliness and has not gained impersonal mobility. The result is, on the one hand, the existence of cliques to compensate for the lack of small-town neighborliness; on the other hand, social inertia based on the· fact that everyone knows who everyone is, where he belongs, and whether he tries to reach beyond himself.

A further force working for conservatism in the city, as in the state as a whole, is the fact that the population is static. The proportion of its inhabitants over forty-five years of age, and even the proportion over sixty-five, is greater than is generally found in the rest of the United States. The youthful energy that makes for change is lacking in its life. Burlington and Vermont, in this respect, have known for almost a hundred years the characteristics of a stationary population toward which the United States as a whole is rapidly tending.

The proportion of foreign-born and those of mixed and foreign parentage is practically the same for the city as for the state as a whole. This proportion has also varied little in eighty years. The foreign-born comprise 12 per cent of the population of the city, as of the state; and those of foreign or mixed parentage 27.5 per cent of the population of the city as compared with 22.8 per cent of the population of the state. In some sections of the state, of course, the old Yankee stock is more nearly intact than, for example, in the northern section, where large areas have been almost completely taken over by the French Canadians.

Here again Burlington typifies the state as a whole, for the largest single immigrant group in the city is the French-Canadian.

Certain factors accentuate the cleavages that exist between these ethnic groups. Tradition is one of them. From the earliest days of America, the Vermonter has had an ingrained distrust of the foreigner. For this reason, when the rest of America was swept along by the conscious effort to assimilate the new elements, Vermont lagged behind. Grudgingly it accepted the fact that it had alien groups in its midst, and by tacit agreement these groups followed separate courses and met only for solving important community problems. Today, when the United States as a whole is being forced by new alignments to meet the basic problems of our civilization on other fronts, one of Vermont's chief community concerns is still the securing of effective coöperation of its ethnic groups for community enterprises while they maintain separate and amicable relations in other aspects of its life.

A further accentuation of cleavages is occasioned by the religious situation in Burlington, arising in part from the fact that the Catholic and the Protestant groups in the community are fairly evenly balanced. This division of the community is enhanced by the presence, on the one hand, of many Catholic institutions, especially the headquarters of the Catholic See of Vermont, and on the other hand, of the University of Vermont. The University is a public institution, but in contradistinction to the Catholic colleges near at hand it is Protestant in tone. As the Old

American Protestant group retreats from commercial power in the city, the last stronghold of its traditions will be on the campus.

The University itself adds new distinctions to those already existing, for although it may have a liberalizing effect upon the theories of its students, in relation to the community as a whole it serves to crystallize cleavages. One of these is, of course, the usual one of town versus gown, of practical versus theoretical men, while another is the separation of those who have attended the local college, perhaps acquired the additional allegiance of a fraternity, from those whose only college was the town's elementary school — a separation emphasized by the large number of college alumni associations attracted to the community by its many educational institutions.

In spite of this atypical accentuation of cleavages, the pattern of life in Burlington is a significant demonstration of the forces which are at work in American communities similar in character. In studying the behavior of such a community we see the problems that face America as a whole as they are met by a culture relatively stable and sympathetic to slow evolutionary change rather than to the greater violence of revolution. Against the background of such a culture, and in the light of the way Burlington has faced and is facing the problem of incorporating its various ethnic groups, we may see the extent to which rural America is united in the pursuit of common aims, and also whether those aims are common enough so that such a community may face strongly the challenge of a changing world.

CHAPTER III

THE MYTH OF A YANKEE TOWN

WALKING along the streets of Burlington, the visitor sees nothing in the appearance of the citizens to remind him of the not-too-distant past when the shawl or apron of a foreigner was a usual part of an American street scene. The women he sees dress in identical styles of similar materials, wear their lipstick in the same way, and have the same swirl in their new permanent waves; the men, too, dress alike, in casual suits not too carefully pressed. Nor does their activity give any impression of cleavages in the community, of barriers separating group from group. On a Saturday night, for example, with stores open until nine or half-past, the citizens of Burlington, the farmers from the country, and visitors from near-by towns, all mingle together. They are going to a Saturday movie, doing last-minute shopping, or just being downstreet with the crowd. It is the end of the working week and there is a relaxed, carefree buoyancy about the group as they go in and out of the chain stores, department stores, five-and-ten-cent stores, along the main street. They rub shoulders together, give a cheery greeting, stop for a few minutes' visit, laugh over the jostlings of the crowd. In this moment of common activity they all bear the stamp of Americans.

But to a Yankee farmer they are not all alike. To him Burlington has a lot of foreigners. As he walks along the main street, he looks in vain for a few faces which remind him of the features of Calvin Coolidge. Going into a store he may be greeted by a proprietor whose short and stocky build little resembles the long, lean Yankee storekeeper of earlier days. While waiting to be served he may listen abstractedly to an animated conversation between the clerk and a customer only to realize suddenly that he is listening to a foreign language. "French," he probably decides, as he turns to give his order. He goes into another store to be waited on by the Jewish proprietor, and comes out a little fearful lest he may have met his match in bargaining. If he stays in town for lunch, he will have to look hard along the main street to find a restaurant which is not Greek, or Syrian, or Chinese, or run by some other "foreigner." It is only when he goes into the bank that he can breathe easily, knowing that here he is still on Yankee ground.

Burlingtonians themselves are occasionally interested in speculating on the extent to which the city is no longer an Old American community. The Federal Census gives them some picture of the changes: according to the figures of 1930, 40 per cent of the population of 24,789 are either immigrants or children of immigrants, 12 per cent being foreign-born and 28 per cent of foreign or mixed parentage. This group of immigrants and children of immigrants is composed of several elements. The French-Canadian, with 4,895 members, is the largest; it comprises one half of all the people of foreign stock belonging to the first and second generations, and one fifth of all the people of the community. The next largest group is that of English-speaking Canadians, who number some 1,208 persons. The Irish come next with 1,102; and the Russians and Poles (most of whom are Jews) come fourth with 741 persons. Other groups of some size are the English, with 457 members; the Italian, 392; and the German, 309. In addition to these, twenty-nine other nationalities are represented in lesser numbers.

The Census, however, does not tell the whole story, for it does not distinguish the nationality or stock of the grandchildren of immigrants. It is therefore only by a count of the three Catholic parishes — two French-Canadian and one Irish — that a more comprehensive picture may be obtained of the size of the ethnic groups of the city which have been here for more than two generations.

Such a count reveals that the French-Canadian element is much larger than it appears to be from the Census enumeration. By the priests' estimate there are in St. Joseph's, the first French-Canadian parish, some 6,000 souls of French-Canadian stock; in St. Anthony's, some 1,500; and in Cathedral, the English-speaking parish, at least 2,000. Hence, according to this count, the people of French-Canadian stock number approximately 9,500 and comprise almost two fifths of the total population of the city. In Cathedral, the English-speaking parish, there are also some 5,000 persons of Irish stock, and 1,000 Italians, Syrians, and persons of other smaller groups. In this Yankee community, therefore, 15,500 persons, more than three fifths of the population, are members of ethnic groups identified with the Roman Catholic faith; and when to this total is added the Jewish group, numbering 800 persons, the elements foreign to the Old Yankee stock are found to compose 66 per cent of the population of the city.

This does not mean that the remaining 34 per cent is a "pure" Yankee group. Rather, it, too, is composed largely of foreign elements, though of kindred ethnic stocks — English, English Canadians, Germans — with the Old Americans themselves, those of the fourth generation or more in this country, making up an extremely small part of the population of the city. Their ranks are reënforced by the peoples of the related ethnic stocks who are of the Protestant faith, and it is chiefly as Protestants in contrast with Roman Catholics that these form a cohesive group.

The city itself is interested in the whole question from the point of view of the comparative size of each religious, rather than of each ethnic, group. Speculation as to the proportion of Protestants to Catholics is a frequent topic of conversation; an old Protestant Yankee does not like to think that he is being crowded out by these newer peoples of a strange faith, and it is with some apprehension that he estimates that the proportion by now may be 50–50, while an Irish Catholic, interested in the growing strength of the peoples of his communion, estimates the ratio at 60–40 in favor of the Catholic group.

The surprise with which the average Yankee in Burlington greets the information that his community is largely of foreign stock attests the fact that Burlington wasn't always like this and that the change that has come over it came so gradually as to be almost imperceptible. The first settlers, to whom the charter of the town was granted in 1763, were adventurous Yankees who built up a prosperous timber trade with Europe via Lake Champlain and Quebec. Later a few French Canadians came down from across the border, but not until 1812 was there a sufficient number of them, 100, for the Catholic See at Boston to send up a priest to be their pastor. They intruded very little on the community; and it was not until 1849, with the building of the railroads, that some Irishmen came to town and made the Yankees aware that there were "furriners" in the land. The story goes that when two gangs of Irishmen working on the railroads met at Burlington a serious quarrel arose between those from County Cork and those from County Connaught, the upshot of which was that a number quit their jobs rather than work with the Irish from another county, and, finding other work in Burlington, decided to build their homes there.

Between 1860 and 1875 the influx of foreigners increased with the boom in the lumber industry. The demand for laborers brought more French Canadians and Irishmen; by 1880 there was a small colony of Germans; by 1885 there were enough Jews to support a synagogue, and by 1890 a group of Italians had come in to dig sewers, and to build roads at the military post situated five miles from Burlington. In the late nineties Burlington felt the reverberations of the wave of imigration which brought hundreds of new Americans from southeastern Europe: a Greek started a restaurant, a Syrian set up a fruit store.

THE LAKE FRONT IN 1860

A photograph taken when Burlington was the second
largest lumber mart in the world.

Thus by the turn of the century the character of Burlington had altered markedly from that of its early beginnings. The change since then has been slower. The only continuous movement of recent times has been that of the French Canadians, who still come down across the border to find work in the textile mills which were Burlington's last gesture toward becoming an industrial city before it settled into its present character as a commercial and educational center.

The role played by each of the main ethnic groups in the life of the community is in part dictated by its historical place in the development of the city and in part by the essential motivation of the group — what it selects out of American life to make its own, what essentially it contributes to the larger community. In order to appreciate the life of the community and the place of each group in that life, it is necessary to make some analysis of the role of each.

Every community contains its corps of people who consider themselves its charter members. They have determined its nature, created its organizations, fostered its development. In Burlington this corps consists of Old American Protestants — the Yankees, as they still are called. They have always lived here, they love the place, they own it. No matter what changes may come over the city, no matter how far it has lost its early character, they watch over its development and growth with a certain sense of responsibility born of the feeling of proprietorship. This feeling is justified in a sense by the fact that most of the institutions around which the life of the city centers today were founded by their forefathers. These had, immediately upon their settling in 1763, set up a town government and public schools, and, as early as 1791, the University of Vermont. After these agencies symbolic of the principles of free government had been established, they turned their attention to the organization of a religious society, which was formed in 1805. Today the descendants of these Old Americans have to a large extent retreated from the commercial life of the city, but they still control the banks, most of the city's manufacturing, and the University. Furthermore, they have through their institutions, and aided by the fact that the immigrant invasion was never great enough to threaten their position of dominance, set an indelible stamp upon the life of the community. An internationally known writer who returned after years abroad to make his home in the city explained how deeply satisfying it was to find here a town where the spirit of early American democracy still endured; where independence of thought, appreciation of character on the basis of worth — qualities which are fast disappearing from the American scene — still survived. Here among the elm-arched streets he felt as if he were coming back to an early American democratic community in which Emerson might still be living.

The small Old American group has been helped to maintain its predominant position by the strength of its traditional feeling of the racial superiority of the Anglo-Saxon. As one woman, concerned about a more successful interrelationship between the various ethnic groups of the community, explained: "Of course you do believe that the English are the finest people yet produced on earth. You do believe that they have the most admirable human qualities and abilities that any people have ever had!" Interestingly enough, the newer peoples on the whole accept the Old Americans at their own valuation, perhaps partly because the premium placed on conformity to standards already set has not permitted them to value their own standards and interpretations of America. At any rate, they always speak highly of the Old Americans as fine people with superior ability, shrewd business men, and leaders of the community; though some qualify their appreciation by commenting that the Old Americans tend to be snobbish and ingrown, and that they place undue emphasis upon the forms of their culture, which they expect all newer peoples to emulate. The criticism, however, is always good-humoredly qualified by: "But they can't help themselves, you know. A Yankee just is like that. You have to accept that when dealing with him."

Traditions of family and name, of power and influence in the financial and civic life of the community, of race-consciousness, plus a very deep conviction that the Protestant traditions of their forefathers are basically important to the development of free institutions in America, set the Old Americans apart as a group distinct from other people. Within that group there are the usual divisions of classes and cliques, of rich and poor; but the common elements of culture and tradition give an impression of a common unit in relation to other ethnic groups in the community. The Old Americans are charter members; they give a kindly welcome to newcomers, as behooves people of their position, but they expect in return the respect that is due charter members. One who can claim even remote blood connections with any of the group is cordially welcomed without question; he is "one of us," while one who cannot claim such connection is "accepted" only as he obeys the forms and the codes of the group, because, after all, he is "not one of us."

Freed from the kind of economic pressure that is known to a great proportion of the people in the other groups, the Old Americans are concerned primarily with "nice living." Their interests and activities connect them with persons outside the community more than with those within; thus they have broad views, wide interests in the arts, literature, and even international relations. In the community, however, their interest is in keeping their place and their prerogatives; their influence tends to preserve the *status quo* and puts a check on too rapid an invasion from the lower ranks into their society.

The Irish are the leaders of the opposition. With the same fighting spirit that they showed in Ireland against the English, under the banner of their religion and their political party they aggressively assert their difference from the Old Americans and take it upon themselves to champion the rights of the immigrant, casting their lot not with the dominant element but with the "have nots." This role for a people who speak the English language and identify

themselves more or less with the English tradition has
made for a conflicting situation even more complex than
that known to their forefathers in Ireland.

Wherever they have settled in America the Irish have
set up such conflict situations, but nowhere more so than
in New England. Their criticism of all things English and
their loyalty to the Roman Catholic Church went deeply
against the grain of the descendants of the Yankee settlers,
who were proud of their English origin and traditions
and of the independence of religious thought expressed in
Protestantism. As a result, to many Old Americans the
Irish have epitomized differences in social philosophy
which are deeply opposed to the English and Protestant
principles upon which this country's institutions were
built. To be an Irishman — a Papist and a Democrat — is
as a red flag to a bull to many a Puritan Yankee. The
failure of each to appreciate the other or to understand
the principles for which the other stands is the basic
tragedy which disturbs the equanimity of any community
where Irish and Old Americans are found together.

In Burlington also the Irish have assumed the role of
champions of political justice for the newer immigrant
groups and leaders of the Catholic Church in America,
while at the same time they have a strong conviction that
as the Old American political leadership diminishes the
Irish will be the inevitable leaders in the political and civic
life of the community. As one of their leaders pointed
out: "The Yankees today aren't the people that their
fathers were. Their fathers were God-fearing men who

were real leaders. Their sons seem somehow to be going to seed. They don't have the life in them. They don't have their fathers' convictions."

The role chosen by the Irish is beset with many difficulties. On the one hand, the newer elements at times find the leadership of the Irish officious and irksome; on the other hand, the older elements sometimes find them pushing, and carry over from their English forebears a distrust of their dependability. As a whole, however, the Irish are spoken of highly by all groups, with qualifications such as those indicated in the comment: "The Irish are loyal and faithful first to their church, second to their kind. When these obligations have been fulfilled, they make excellent citizens, contributing to the best interests of the community."

The difference between the French Canadians and the other groups in Burlington cannot be understood without a recognition of the attitude with which the French Canadians regard the territory itself. They may not proclaim it from the house-tops, but to them Burlington is a French city and they are its true citizens. To all of New England they have felt a peculiar claim. After all, they say, was it not French explorers and priests who opened up much of the country? Did not Samuel de Champlain discover this very territory, and were not the French the first white settlers on the shores of Lake Champlain? Certainly a military conquest could not entirely take away the feeling that they have a right to this territory. Some of their leaders, at least, have continued to dream of the day when New England will again be New France.

With this belief deep within them, their settling in New England has differed from that of other people. Their migration has been a "peaceful penetration" across an imaginary line; indeed, at first their migration was largely seasonal. Some Burlingtonians still recall the trainloads of French Canadians, through with their work on the farms, who would arrive each fall to work in the lumber yards and mills and after staying for a short season to earn, as they said, some of the gold and silver that America had to offer, would return to their poor Canadian farms. On the farms of Quebec, as in Europe, "The States" was pictured as a land with streets of gold. Gradually they began to lengthen their stay here from one season to two, from two seasons to three; then they came for a period of two or three years, until they settled permanently. When they did, it was not so much like settling in a new land as extending the boundaries of the old. The tie with Canada has always remained strong, partly because the short distance to the home land makes close contact possible, partly because the continued migration without restriction of French Canadians has constantly reënforced the Canadian national spirit.

Although they are French, they differ markedly from the Frenchman of today and are, in habit of thought and behavior, more closely akin to his forebears. They have been separated from France for over 170 years and have known nothing of the great liberalizing movements, such as the French Revolution, the great literary revolution, and other upheavals which have so greatly influenced modern France. Their way of life in Canada has therefore remained essentially that of a simple peasant folk whose most vital cultural element has been their religion; as in any primitive society, the forms of that religion govern every aspect of their lives. This circumstance has made far more for docility and obedience to rules than it has for the quality of individual enterprise and responsibility considered characteristic of America. They have willingly accepted the leadership of the parish priest as their forebears did two centuries ago. In the French-Canadian community around the cotton mill in Burlington, today, the priest is spiritual guide, lawyer, doctor, friend, and comforter, to his people. Such complete acceptance of a single cultural force has resulted, in the estimation of many students, in a lack of interest in other forms of development, a result manifested in the lack of schools and free libraries in French Canada.

In Burlington those of French Canadian descent form a bloc of nearly ten thousand people. Although individually volatile, they are as a group unassertive, concerned primarily with maintaining what they have in the way of national integrity — their religion, their language, their customs. They have never had to fight for these in the same way as the Irish. The right was granted them by the British at the time of the conquest and they have preserved these characteristics by constant passive resistance to outside influence whether British or French. Even in Burlington they seem less perturbed than others by the course of outside events; they put their faith in God and quietly produce the future population of the city.

In contrast with the Old Americans and the Irish, however, as one of their number said, "the French don't stick together. They act as if they felt inferior and ashamed of their nationality. They don't speak up for themselves, and they have nobody to speak up for them. If they had strong leaders, they would be more proud of being French; and that would be good." Their spokesmen in America, sensitive to the fact that the French Canadians have by comparison with other groups contributed but little to America in terms of material success, in all their newspapers point out that French Canadians have a very special contribution to make to American life, a contribution of spiritual rather than material wealth. In the midst of a materialistic world, they say, the French-Canadian group stands for religion, things of the spirit. Admitting that the group will probably never have much of material wealth or power, they point out that the way of poverty is the way to heaven, and that the spiritual mission of the French Canadians is to show materialistic America a way of life which is the way of Jesus.

As a peaceful, unaggressive people, they have won to some extent the sympathy of the Yankee group, whose social and economic position is not threatened by their advancement. This Yankee sympathy is based partly on the belief that they have had to submit to Irish leadership in religious organization and partly on the belief that they have been held back in Canada as a conquered people. There is also in it, however, something of the attitude of an adult to a child, an appreciation of their warm, earthy

simplicity and a delight in the "quaint" aspects of their
behavior, as presented in the poems of Rowland Robin-
son. But this attitude is accompanied by a rejection of
some of the very qualities which make them charming.

The Jews, destined to be dispersed among all peoples on
the face of the earth, have a quota of 800 in Burlington.
With a long history of persecution and suffering behind
them, they have sought to find a place of freedom for the
oppressed. Perhaps the principles on which this country
was based have meant no more to any group than to the
Jews. The intensity of feeling may be seen in part by the
remark of one Jewish woman who said: "The first thing
I did when I came to America was to kiss the ground.
This was a free land — my country. Here there would
be no more pogroms."

In Burlington they have pursued the dual role the Jews
have had to assume in America as much as in any other
country. On the one hand much of their life is within the
group, centered around the synagogue and the Talmud
Torah, for even in America, though they may enjoy
equality before the law, they know discrimination born of
prejudices ingrained for centuries in the Gentile mind. On
the other hand, showing their appreciation of the liberty
that America offers, they actively participate in all civic
and philanthropic enterprises. In Burlington their presence
is being more and more felt, and some people worry that
their influence is becoming an irritant in the life of the
community; but their role essentially is that of the impersonal outsider whose support is sought in times of intra-

community conflict between the two main branches of the Christian faith.

The Germans have nearly as much right as the Yankees to the claim of first citizens of Burlington. When Ira Allen came in 1773 he found two Germans settled on the shores of Shelburne Point. According to Allen, they "had the appearance of peaceable men, and on their promise to behave were suffered to remain undisturbed." Whether because of this "peaceableness" or because their numbers have never been large, the Germans have quickly become almost indistinguishable from the rest of the community. Today they number 300 persons, but it was not until 1880 that enough of them found their way from the surrounding towns to form a little German neighborhood in the city. Those who came were largely from one section of the country, Silesia, where they had been farmers, weavers, and artisans; in Burlington they fitted into the lumber mills and trades. The German love of music, of intellectual discussions, and especially of *Gemutlichkeit* led them to organize as early as 1891 a German club, a branch of the National Order of Harugari, which is still the center of German social life in the town. It aims to preserve and transmit to the second and third generation an appreciation of German culture.

Two Italians reached Burlington in 1890. A few years later, while working under their padrones on the Delaware and Hudson Railroad on the New York side of the lake, some came over in search of a suitable location for their families. When they found that in Burlington they

could secure work in building some of the streets and
sewers, they decided to settle. For some time, while there
was work on the roads and in building the near-by army
post, there were more Italians in Burlington than there
are at present. Now, though few in number, they are not
a compact group — the three or four families from northern Italy distinguishing themselves from the majority who
have come from the southern part. Unlike the Irish or the
French Canadians, they have made no effort to center
their life around a church of their own. This is due partly
to their small number, but also partly to traditions of a
state-supported church which make Italians slow to establish and support a church of their own. They are more or
less lost in the English-speaking parish; and only at times
of baptisms, funerals, and marriages do they feel the need
of seeking the services of a French-Canadian priest who
is well versed in Italian. In 1934, for the first time, they
organized an Italian club. This has been an important
social center for all the Italians in Burlington and Winooski, and an educational force aiming to make them feel at
home in America and understand its ways and laws.

Representatives of other peoples have added their peculiar qualities to Burlington, but they are too few to form
distinctive groups, or they have already fused into the
larger blend. The English and English Canadians, with
traditions so similar to those of the Old Americans, have
merged with that group. Syrians and Greeks, part of the
last great migration from southeastern Europe, are few in
number. The Syrians comprise some thirty families, the

first of whom came to Burlington in 1895; they have established no church of their own but have become members of the English-speaking Roman Catholic parish; their unity is expressed through the social activities of the Lady of Mount Lebanon Society. The Greeks number some twenty families, or 130 persons; one or two Greeks were in Burlington in 1902 in small fruit stores and restaurants. The Greeks remain individualistic, and come together as a group only on special occasions, as when a Greek Orthodox priest comes to town; ordinarily they attend the Episcopal Church, which has been the most hospitable to them as well as nearest in teaching to their own. The American Hellenic Educational Patriotic Association is an important force in uniting all the Greeks of Vermont, emphasizing pride in the Greek heritage. Other people, such as Norwegians, Swedes, Finns, Armenians, Turks, Negroes, and some representatives of seventeen other nationality groups, are too few in number to do much more than add a touch of color to the pageant of peoples who have found their way to Burlington.

The life of all these people is the story of the process of becoming at home in the ever-changing, increasingly complex, American world. They are all intent on realizing the hopes and dreams which America has symbolized to them or their forebears. Each group, according to its need, clings to its customs and traditions as to things assured in an unsure world; each has had to realize that this country has welcomed not only its own group but also those that have been its traditional enemies. Only slowly has each realized that the large economic and social forces affecting all America are drawing them all together in common concerns: all are concerned with earning a living, bringing up their children, keeping up their religious practices; all hope that their children may realize what they did not enjoy; all hope for a little fun; all worry over their old age.

In the process of adjusting to their new American environment, different potentialities within the groups have been brought out — special interests in educational training, in the kinds of jobs they have taken. Thus, slowly, new divisions are arising within the groups; and those with similar interests have begun to reach across barriers of nationality or religion which once were all-important in American life. New divisions are being formed. The old, however, those of nationality or religion, may often color these new developments, especially as each group has not fully realized the sense of freedom that it hoped to find in America.

In Burlington it is possible to observe the advances and checks experienced by each group in its attempt to share in the common life of the community and to see therein the part that these early differences in America play in the new cleavages which inevitably form in a more settled society. It is possible to see the advantages and the disadvantages of preserving the old lines against the rapid social change in the world about us.

CHAPTER IV

HUMAN GEOGRAPHY

FIVE o'clock is a rush hour even in Burlington. From offices and factories people pour into the streets and hurry homeward, stopping only for a moment to buy a newspaper from a shouting newsboy on the corner. They hurry across the town, up or down the hill, until shortly after six o'clock quiet reigns over the business section of the city.

The rush homeward is merely a reshuffling of a patch-work design. As each man sits down with his family to the supper table his home becomes part of a pattern very similar to that of the working day. If he is a French-Canadian mill worker, his neighbors are other French Canadians, with a sprinkling of Irish, Jews, one or two Italians, a Syrian. If he is a Yankee paying teller in the bank, his neighbors will be Yankees, interspersed with a few Irish and a very small representation of newer peoples.

The lines which separate "good" neighborhoods from "bad" are distinct, and the people who live in one neighborhood are unlikely to know those who live in another. It is, for example, a long mile, in terms of social distance, that separates those who live at the foot of the hill — a region of wharves and warehouses, shabby tenements and railroad tracks — from those who live on its upper slope. Social separation is further demarcated by

Pearl Street, the old trail running down the slope of the hill, which in earlier times connected the other settlements of the state with the little colony of Burlington Bay. Generally speaking, to live north of Pearl Street, and especially on the lower slope of the hill, is to live at a distance not measurable by any measuring rod from those who reside south of Pearl Street, and especially on the upper slope of the hill. Although the waterfront has been the first home of each group, as each has bettered its circumstances it has moved up the slope and, in recent times, southward, until the houses near the waterfront which have sheltered in succession tenants of every nationality have been left harboring the least successful of each group.

The political divisions of the city — the wards — follow to some extent the same pattern. Wards 2 and 3 reach north from Pearl Street; Ward 4 runs along the waterfront. These are looked upon as "foreign" wards, where French Canadian, German, Irishman, and Jew live as next-door neighbors. Ward 1 includes the top of the hill and its Winooski slope; Ward 5 includes the center of the city; Ward 6, the southern sections. Except for the isolated area around the mills at the lower end of Ward 6, these wards are looked upon by the Old Americans as "pure," their own, since here Old America is represented to a greater extent than elsewhere in the city.

Actually, of course, economic status is the most important single factor in determining choice of residence: people of each ethnic group are to be found in all wards,

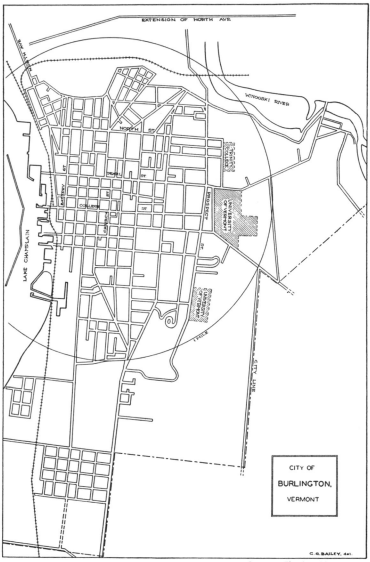

EXTENSION OF NORTH AVE

WINOOSKI RIVER

LAKE CHAMPLAIN

NORTH ST

TRINITY COLLEGE

UNIVERSITY OF VERMONT

UNIVERSITY OF VERMONT

1 MILE

CITY LINE

CITY OF
BURLINGTON,
VERMONT

C. G. BAILEY, del.

Courtesy Fleming Museum

from the poorest to the finest residential sections; but within an area of comparable economic land and rent values, there is a tendency for neighborhoods to form along ethnic lines. Thus, for example, although the majority of the newer peoples are to be found in Wards 2, 3, and 4, a spot map of the city reveals a certain ethnic patchwork pattern even within this section.

The French Canadians are found primarily in two sections of the city; 28 per cent of the first- and second-generation householders inhabit the extreme southern part of the town on the outskirts of Ward 6, in the neighborhood of the factories and mills where they work; 59 per cent live in Wards 2, 3, and 4, concentrated largely in the northern sections where they first settled. The remainder are fairly evenly scattered throughout the other two wards. The Jewish group, very early in the history of its settlement, moved from the waterfront to a distant northern section of the community because of the desire, some of its leaders explain, to be apart from other peoples. There the Jews are located in a wedge-shaped section of streets, parts of Ward 2 and Ward 3; more than half of them are concentrated in a small area in Ward 2, almost a quarter in Ward 3. The consequence is that although many French Canadians and people of other nationalities live in this neighborhood, it is looked upon as the Jewish section of the city. The remaining Jews are scattered principally through the better residential sections of Wards 1 and 6. More than half of the Germans reside in a small section of Ward 4 around the German clubhouse; the remainder are scattered fairly evenly through the other wards of the city. Almost half of the Italians live in a narrow area near the foot of the hill in the central part of town where Wards 4 and 5 meet; they are especially clustered in a square of four blocks. Another Italian neighborhood is at the foot of the eastern slope of the hill where Burlington joins Winooski; here one fourth of the Italians are to be found. The remainder are dispersed throughout the better residential sections of the city. Fairly well dispersed through all the wards are the Irish, yet slightly more than half of them live in the "wards of the melting pot," where they are settled along the entire slope of the hill — north of Pearl Street, it is true, but south of the main body of French Canadians and Jews. The Old Americans live primarily in Wards 5, 6, and 1 — the "pure" wards, of which the "purest" section is the upper slope of the hill, with the University as its focal center.

The neighborhood pattern changes but little from generation to generation. French Canadians of the second generation live in much the same neighborhoods as first-generation French Canadians, and the same is true for each of the other groups. Yet where a group has spread out, the movement is usually of second-generation representatives. The greater proportion of the Irish and the Jews in the so-called "pure" wards are of the second generation.

This division of the city into different ethnic areas roughly coinciding with the different economic areas tends to perpetuate itself. A French-Canadian woman explained her lack of desire to move by telling of a friend of hers who had moved into an Old American neighborhood: "What has she got? She's up there, where she wanted to be, she thinks she's living with those people. But she's not, she's living alone, and I don't want to live alone." Wherever invisible lines separate the homes of the older and the newer elements, attitudes of superiority and inferiority are easily cultivated; the neighborhood not only derives some of its character from its inhabitants but also stamps its inhabitants with some of its own quality. The newer elements to be found in the slums are looked down upon because of the neighborhood in which they live, yet when one of them moves into a better residential section he arouses resentment. That he is "getting beyond himself" is a belief shared by those whom he has left behind and those whose territory he has invaded. As a result of this attitude, he frequently feels that the change isn't worth while, and this feeling acts as a deterrent to mobility.

But the fact that different ethnic groups have lived together for a long time at about the same economic level, as in the melting-pot wards, does not prove that they want each other for neighbors. Wherever different groups live in close proximity they develop marked likes and dislikes of each other. An individual whose personality is unpleasant may serve to intensify in the minds of his neighbors prejudicial attitudes against the ethnic group of which he is considered representative, while another with more attractive characteristics may find that the prejudicial attitudes toward his race are so well established in the minds of his neighbors that he is rejected by them before he has a chance to demonstrate his individual quality. Only rarely do people achieve the objectivity toward the neighbors expressed by the Italian who said, "Any one who tends to his business while I tend to mine is a good neighbor; there is good and bad in all nationalities." Seldom do they pass beyond evaluation in other terms to the other considerations indicated by the words of one Old American who said, "I would rather have an energetic Jew as a neighbor any time than a gone-to-seed Yankee."

The answers to the question "whom do you prefer as a neighbor?" throw considerable light on the problem of ethnic amalgamation as it is exemplified in this field of neighborhood selection. Almost invariably the persons questioned in detailed interviews expressed a preference for members of their own ethnic groups as neighbors; the newer peoples' second choice was usually the Old American group, and their third choice the Irish, while at the bottom of the list were placed the Negroes and the Chinese. Although the persons questioned were apathetic toward many groups concerning whom they knew little, they nevertheless rejected the Chinese and the Negroes of whom they knew no more, basing this condemnation not on any qualities or characteristics of these groups, but on the generalization that Chinese were after all Chinese, and Negroes, Negroes.

The position given to the English Canadians casts an

interesting reflection on the general preference for Old Americans. The Old Americans preferred English Canadians as neighbors second only to themselves, because, as they said, "They are like our own people." The newer elements, however, although they preferred Old Americans second to their own people, put the English Canadians well down the list along with Syrians, Greeks, and Italians, or among other peoples concerning whom they would express no opinion because "they didn't know them." The preference for the Old Americans, therefore, would not seem necessarily to indicate a real liking for their essential characteristics, but rather a desire on the part of the newer peoples to identify themselves with those elements of the community which they think are the most American in American life.

These prejudices and preferences may remain latent until a situation arises which calls them into action. When, for example, a member of a newer ethnic group moves into a neighborhood which the inhabitants feel is their own and exclusive, the latent attitudes are focused and given overt expression. If he is, for example, an English Canadian moving onto the slope of the hill among the Old Americans, the predisposition is to welcome him. If, however, he is a Jew, even though of comparable background, he is more likely to be held suspect from the beginning. Indeed, an inhabitant of these exclusive neighborhoods who wishes to sell or rent his home is usually extremely careful to find as a tenant a member of a group acceptable to his neighbors.

The feeling against a Jew's either renting or buying a house in the better neighborhoods is an extreme example of this kind of discrimination. Against him the usual prejudice is augmented by jealousy; both newer and older elements resent, consciously or unconsciously, the fact that the Jews get ahead faster than do other groups and are quicker to insist on building their homes in good neighborhoods. Thus in some sections of Burlington, as in many other cities, it is impossible for a Jew to buy property or to rent a home. Many Old Americans share the feeling of the one who explained: "If a Jew moves in, the value of the surrounding property goes down. It's just bad business to let them come. The same is true of apartment houses. If you want some tenants who are not Jews, you cannot have any Jewish tenants." That actually there is no instance in Burlington of this kind of wholesale movement of the Jews into a neighborhood where one Jew has moved has not dissipated the fear that it would occur. The first Jew to move into a neighborhood is still considered the entering wedge of a potential invasion, although some shrewd Yankees have pointed out that it has frequently been a good policy to let one selected Jew into a neighborhood. "He's likely to be a lot more cautious than the rest of us about letting another Jew in for fear the other Jew won't have the characteristics we like. Besides, he knows more about them."

These prejudicial attitudes, however, are not the only check placed upon the mobility of an ambitious member of a new group. His own people, after he has moved on, tend to make him feel that he has deserted them, can never again be identified with them in quite the same old way. Nothing can express this attitude better than the scornful words of one old Irish woman who referred to some of her compatriots who had moved into better neighborhoods as "lace-curtain Irish."

This, then, is part of the complex of factors, social and economic, which tends to stabilize the system of neighborhoods and so to postpone the achievement of a unified community. Yet it must be remembered that there are two aspects of such a division. By living in a neighborhood composed mostly of persons of like heritage and interests, the individual can enjoy the secure feeling of "belonging" to a world which, however limited its horizons, however petty its jealousies and irritations, has a friendly quality. As one Italian explained: "We could have moved up on the hill. Joe was offered a job as janitor in one of the houses and we would have gotten an apartment for pay. But we walked up there the other day, and it looked so lonely. There wasn't a person in the streets. They were even too classy to sit out on their porches. Here folks are always passing by and coming in to visit with me. I like folks. If we were up there, our friends from down here wouldn't come up to see us and those people wouldn't come in to see us, so we're staying here."

The need that such persons feel for a secure and friendly atmosphere is a factor in preventing any great mobility in the community. In fact, it results in a resistance to change and, in its more acute forms, a social inertia stultifying in the extreme. When such a condition prevails, it is only the person with extraordinary will who is able to move out of his narrow orbit and face a larger and more impersonal world. It takes, further, an alert person to recognize that the "impersonal" quality he meets may be a trend of the times and not, as he is likely to believe, an indication that the group into which he has moved doesn't want him. True, the new group may not want him, being as conservative as his own group, but in a community such as Burlington nationality and racial prejudices serve primarily to enhance prejudices of class born of economic and social differences.

What, then, is the chance for change? Do the people of the community favor neighborhoods which are separated along ethnic lines? In the light of the fact that such neighborhoods tend to preserve barriers between group and group, the answer to this question is a significant indication of the possibilities for building a people united above ethnic differences.

Opinion in Burlington, ascertained by means of attitude scales given to the 459 persons who were interviewed in detail, revealed that in general people do not wish to maintain distinct neighborhoods, although many of those questioned expressed a desire for some degree of segregation as a means of preserving their particular culture and traditions. Almost two thirds of the 447 people who expressed an opinion on this matter indicated that the preservation of nationality neighborhoods was of little or no interest to them. They were imbued with a belief in the American tradition of "getting ahead," and they wanted no check upon their freedom to move into another neighborhood if they should so wish. A little more than a quarter of them wished to maintain free mobility while preserving something of a nationality neighborhood in order to keep alive the cultural heritage of their people. Less than one tenth favored distinct nationality neighborhoods as a significant factor in preserving ethnic identity. The extent to which the people questioned were opposed to rigid nationality neighborhoods indicates the part played by social and economic factors in maintaining the ethnic patchwork pattern in Burlington's life. There was, however, a considerable difference of opinion among certain groups.

Despite the reputation of the French Canadians for clannishness, one half of the 139 persons interviewed considered that little or no effort should be made to preserve a distinct French-Canadian neighborhood. Some of them felt this way because they believed that very little, if any, French-Canadian culture should be distinctly preserved. Others adopted this point of view as a concession to the actual situation. "It would be good," said one French Canadian, "if the French would live together so they would not forget their language or customs, but it can't be done. The higher class French don't like to live with the other French; there are lots of French I wouldn't look at and lots that wouldn't associate with me. It's the money that counts as to how and where you live." The remaining French, however, were more conservative. Almost a third chose the middle way of considerable dispersal while preserving something of a neighborhood so that interest could be equally divided between French-Canadian interests and those of the large community. Only 6 per cent favored complete segregation; but an additional 13 per cent, while not considering segregation essential, believed that interests should be focused almost entirely within one's own nationality group.

This conservatism of the French Canadians can be matched only by that of the Old Americans. Their attitude revealed the conflict between an emotional reaction against inroads of strange people with strange customs and an intellectual appreciation of a sense of responsibility toward newer peoples. Twenty of the ninety-eight Old Americans interviewed favored living in a separate neighborhood and devoting most of their interests and activities to their own group. This conservative group, although only 1 per cent larger than the comparable group among the French Canadians, was much more emphatic than the same group among the French Canadians in insisting on the need of maintaining a distinct nationality neighborhood for themselves. Their desire for exclusiveness was based on such reasons as the following: "There are so many foreigners that we are better off by ourselves. They could never mingle in this town. They are too entirely different." "Perhaps it is not for the best for the whole community, but it seems to be the natural course. The Old Americans are happier by themselves." A number of Old Americans felt that the Yankees should remain separate, from the newer peoples, "not as a nationality group but as a class."

In contrast to this conservatism, a greater proportion of the Old Americans than of any other group expressed the most liberal attitudes. Sixty-one of the ninety-eight interviewed favored the free intermingling of all peoples in the community with little or no emphasis on distinct racial neighborhoods as a means of maintaining ethnic integrity; only seventeen placed equal emphasis on living with their own group and intermingling with the others. "I think," explained one who had adopted the more liberal attitude, "that no one culture is important. It will be the composite culture of all which will make the American of two or three generations hence, and so we should intermingle freely." "We mustn't," elaborated another, "button up Old American culture by segregating it. We must rub it up and polish it off against the other fellows. Our culture should be able to stand it."

The Irish, the Germans, and the Italians expressed the most liberal points of view. Eighty of the eighty-three Irish, thirty-one of the thirty-two Germans, and twenty-eight of the thirty-nine Italians interviewed believed in dispersion leading ultimately to complete or almost complete assimilation. The amazingly high proportion of the first two groups holding this opinion is a measure of the extent to which these peoples feel identified with America, while that of the last is partly wish fulfillment and partly the result, as one Italian explained, of the size of the group in Burlington: "We're too small to be alone. We have to spread out. Maybe if we were as large a group as they have in New York we'd stay more separate."

The attitude of the Jews was influenced by their experience of the past. Remembering the ghetto, they are opposed to any form of segregation and were emphatic about their feeling that people should be free to live wherever they wish. Even among the forty-four (of fifty-six interviewed) who believed that Jews should devote as much interest to their own group as to the community at large, few felt that there was any need to live in a distinct community. Yet many of them recognized the realities of the situation. "I believe in complete fusion," said one man, "but people are not ready for the idea. Meanwhile one must take a compromising point of view and decide to keep something which one can call one's own." The bitter experience which must have gone into the creation of such an acceptant attitude is indicated by the remark of an old Jewish woman who said, "People should not live where they are not wanted. A 'good morning' from a neighbor counts."

Thus it is to be seen that though to a large extent neighborhood divisions on an ethnic basis do exist, they are not necessarily desired. Primarily they are an expression of variance in economic status, which takes the form of separation along ethnic lines because, as will be indicated in the following chapter, the industrial and economic pattern of the community is largely laid out along ethnic lines. If an Irishman, for example, lives in a poor neighborhood, it is more because he is poor than because he is

Irish, although this is least true of the Jew, whose freedom of movement is limited more than that of other
people by prejudice.

Even in Burlington, where consciousness of ethnic separation is still an important element in division, the economic forces affecting the rest of the world are at work,
slowly breaking down the ethnic divisions and revealing
the economic and class divisions at their base. To the casual eye, perhaps, the good neighborhood of today looks
very little different from that of twenty years ago. The
large houses are still there and the lawns surrounding
them are still, for the most part, as wide. Yet looking
more closely one can see that more and more of the houses
have either the Greek letters of a college fraternity above
their doors or have been turned into apartments. On
some of the wide lawns too, small, shiny new houses are
rising to shelter a newer people. They don't belong there,
say the Old Americans; they're not the right kind of
houses. The people in them are strange and think differently. But there they are and they help to pay the taxes.
In time, perhaps, it will be forgotten that they weren't
always there. Thus the ethnic complexion of even Burlington's hill is changing.

These tendencies have not progressed very far, however, and on the lower economic levels they are not expressed so much in geographical redistribution as in a
changing attitude between those who always have lived
together. As one Italian woman expressed it: "Of course
we don't like the French; Italians never have; it's in the

blood. But here they are and here we are, and as long as both of us can pay only fifteen dollars a month rent we'll live next to each other, so what's the good of fighting over whether the French or the Italians are better?"

CHAPTER V

THE PATTERN OF THE WORKING WORLD

THERE are three distinct strata in Burlington's working world. Geographically they are located at three levels on the slope of the hill. People either go to work in the factories, warehouses, and lumber yards that stretch in a long line at the foot of the hill and parallel to the lake; or they go to business in the stores, shops, and offices of the main business section halfway up the hill; or they go to teaching in the University at the top of the hill or to the day's task in some other professional office.

Wherever they work the common concern of all is in making a living, for the community can boast few families wealthy enough to be free of this necessity; but earning a living is expressed in somewhat different terms for those who work at the various levels. To the majority of the workmen in the mills and factories, the primary concern is: Will the job hold out? Will it be a slack season? Shall I be able to pay the doctor's bill and buy new shoes for the children? In recent years only a few have been able to venture beyond this to the question: Shall I get ahead?

To the clerks and office workers on Church Street, this concern means rather: Shall I be able to get that dress Mary wants for the party next week? How am I going to meet that insurance premium next month? To the business man on the same geographic level but on a higher economic one, the questions are often in larger terms: Shall I be able to turn in my car for a new one and take the family on a summer trip to the Middle West? Can I afford to buy the new fixtures and furnishings my wife wants for the house? If business is bad, his question may be: Should I undertake a big loan to tide me over till better times? At the top of the hill, the man who makes a living is concerned with stretching a meager salary to keep up a position and place in the community befitting a college professor: How, on this salary, am I going to be able to send my boy to Yale or Harvard? Ought I to cancel that Easter vacation trip to New York? the money saved could go toward dancing lessons for the children or for two weeks at a summer camp.

These main divisions of Burlington's citizens into working class, business class, and professional class, as in all other parts of America where immigrant groups are numerous, are enhanced by various ethnic distinctions. It is in the American tradition that the ranks of the working class have been continuously recruited from the newer arrivals, and that as they take their places in the least desirable jobs the older inhabitants move up the scale into the preferred positions. As soon as each group does so, it quickly forgets the lowly tasks it once performed and identifies each new group with the type of work it does first, looking upon its members with increasing superiority as "dagos," wops," or "frogs." This tendency to identify each ethnic group with a job is increased by the fact that, though some members of the group may advance more quickly and farther than others, the group as a whole is apt to form a solid bloc in an industry. Thus the French Canadians are identified with the cotton and woolen mills of New England, the Poles with iron foundries, the Italians with road-building and ditch-digging, the Greeks with restaurants, the Chinese with laundries. American industry is a patchwork pattern of nationality groups.

This ethnic patchwork pattern within the main divisions of working class and business class has far-reaching consequences. In a mobile society such as that of America, the job one holds is the most important single index of social and economic status. It determines the neighborhood in which one lives, what people one may associate with, and what clubs one may join. But when, in addition, whole occupations are identified with certain ethnic groups, the job is still further restrictive in determining one's neighborhood, friends, and acquaintances in terms of ethnic as well as economic acceptability. Members of each ethnic group discover, even in the second and third generation, that their social rating in the community is determined in large part by the occupations pursued by the majority of their members. Thus, in order to understand the relationship between the ethnic groups in other aspects of community life, it is important to know the place they hold in the work-a-day world.

In Burlington the ethnic patchwork may not be so strictly marked as in large industrial centers where there are many different nationalities, but the same general design prevails. It is sufficiently evident for a stranger visiting the factories and mills to conclude that Burlington is a French city, while if, seeking a lawyer or a physician, he were to go through the list of professional men in the community, he would be equally convinced that he was in a Yankee community. Although representatives of every nationality are to be found in every occupation in the city, certain rough divisions of labor along nationality lines appear. The following illustrations are based largely on the city directory.

The laboring jobs and the factory and mill work are largely done by representatives of the newer elements, but even among these there is a definite selective process at work. In the mills and factories, for example, employers estimate that from 80 to 95 per cent of the laborers are of French-Canadian stock — an estimate borne out by the findings of the preliminary survey, which revealed that of all householders employed in the mills 75 per cent were of French-Canadian descent. Undoubtedly the unmarried individuals would raise this percentage considerably. The slight sprinkling of other nationalities, each representing only 2 to 6 per cent of the total, helps to support the belief that mill work is almost exclusively the domain of the French Canadians.

Further up the economic scale, in the world of the tradesmen and middlemen, there is no similar domination by any one group. Here still, however, the French Canadians form a large bloc. For example, thirty-six of the fifty-nine barbers in the community are of French-Canadian stock and four are of French extraction. The Old Americans, their nearest competitors, lag far behind with only six barbers. Among bakers, French Canadians are also in the lead, claiming seven of the twenty bakers in the city. Even among grocers, where competition is keen, with fifteen nationalities in the running, the French Canadians are in the lead, with thirty-two of the 117 grocers; competition with the Old Americans becomes closest here, however, since twenty grocers belong to the latter group.

When it comes to the professions, the whole picture changes. The lead at once taken by the Old Americans in all the professions increases rapidly in those which demand longest training and have the greatest social traditions. Thus among the physicians and surgeons, the Old Americans are represented by thirty-two, or more than half of the sixty listed. The Irish assume second place with sixteen, or a little more than a quarter, and the French Canadians fall back to a representation of only four. The English Canadians with four, the English and Scottish with one each, and the Jews with two, comprise the rest of the group. Among the lawyers, the Old Americans again outdistance any other group, contributing thirty-one of the forty-four lawyers in the city. Their nearest rivals are the Irish and the Jews, with only four representatives each; the French Canadians are even farther in the rear, with only two lawyers; while the English, English Canadians, and Syrians each are represented by one.

This main design in Burlington's working world is, of course, not static. The will to "get on," to achieve, to make a name for oneself, is a powerful force that affects the proportional representation of the various groups at each occupational level. There is a continual striving to rise from unskilled to skilled labor, from laboring to white-collar jobs. But the very rate of advance differs from group to group in such a way as to help to preserve the basic pattern.

The most outstanding advances have been made by the Jews and the Irish. The progress of the Irish within the ranks of labor has been described by one railroad official as follows: "Where forty years ago the Irish were the laborers on the railroads, today they are its conductors and officials. Among other workmen they are now the foremen and overseers." Their marked shift away from domestic and personal service is evident from the analysis of the occupations of 159 first- and second-generation Irish householders. The decrease from 29 per cent of the first-generation householders engaged in this service to 13 per cent of the second has undoubtedly continued into the third generation. This, of course, is in direct line with a marked decline everywhere in the number of domestic servants, but in every field the Irish show a line of advance from the laboring and unskilled jobs to the white-collar jobs. In trade, for example, 22 per cent of the second generation are engaged, as compared with 7 per cent of the first. Two members of the second generation are even listed among bank officials and trustees, which positions have until recently been the exclusive domain of the Old Americans.

In their representation in clerical occupations and professions, the Irish, together with the English Canadians, lead all other immigrant groups; in each of these fields the Irish are represented by 8 per cent of their number; with one exception these are of the second generation.

The progress of the Jews has been characteristic. They aim always to be independent, whether they are artisans, business men, or professional men. They form a distinct bloc in some occupations and have no representation in others, circumstances due in large part to the limited range of choice that they have known either in the Old World or in America. They have, however, taken advantage of the freedom which America offers to make conspicuous progress in their occupations, and they strive to provide for their children advantages denied for themselves. Their advance is summarized in the grudging comment of an Old American woman: "I can remember twenty-five years ago when the only Jews I ever saw in Burlington were peddlers with beards and funny clothes, calling out for old clothes along the streets. But today the Jews are in all kinds of business. They even own stores on Church Street, and they dress just as well as you or I, if not better."

The rapid advance of the second generation, as indicated by an analysis of the occupations of 150 first- and second-generation Jewish householders, makes clear this tendency. No member of the second generation of Jews is a peddler or a huckster, although a few of the first generation still are; only 14 per cent of the second generation, as compared with 29 per cent of the first, are employed in manufacturing or mechanical industries, and all so engaged are independent artisans, such as tailors, painters, or bakers. In the professions the Jews have made advances with which the progress of no other group can compare. Although only 7 per cent of the total group are engaged in professions, the proportion of the second generation so engaged is 14 per cent, as compared with 5 per cent of the first. Moreover, while those of the first generation in the professions are rabbis and teachers within their own group, those of the second are lawyers and physicians identified with the community as a whole.

In marked contrast with the rapid advance of the Irish and the Jews is the slower progress of the French Canadians; 59 per cent of 847 first- and second-generation French-Canadian householders are employed either as unskilled or skilled laborers in the manufacturing and mechanical industries, yet whereas seven out of every ten of the first generation are employed either as laborers and operators in the cotton or woolen mills, or as painters, carpenters, and other laborers, only five out of every ten of the second generation are so employed.

There is a complementary increase in the proportional representation of the French Canadians in occupations higher in the scale. For example, in domestic and personal service, an occupation sometimes considered higher than that of the laborer in that it places greater personal responsibility upon the individual, 11 per cent of the second generation are engaged as against only 5 per cent of the first. But even though the French are taking the place of the Irish in domestic service, they do not any more than any other group look upon it as a desirable permanent occupation. Domestic service is not yet on the level where individuals can have the same sense of feeling of independence that they have in other work. The comment of a French-Canadian girl probably voices the opinion of a large number: "You do housework and you're never free. They expect you to work all the time and stay in the house. When you work in the mill you just work seven hours and you are through. You are free to go your own way and you get better pay too."

The shift toward white-collar jobs is gradual but definite; for example, 17 per cent of the second generation are engaged in trade as against only 11 per cent of the first. Only 2 per cent of all the French-Canadian householders are in the professions, but here more than twice as many are of the second generation as of the first.

Many conjectures have been made as to the reason for this slow advance of the French-Canadian group. Some are convinced that it is due to lower average intelligence of the group as a whole. Others speculate that it is due to their whole social heritage, which has not encouraged them to take advantage of educational opportunities or to make ambitious advances in occupational pursuits. An observation in this respect made by a citizen who belongs to the fourth generation of French and Irish stock and who has lived many years in the city is interesting: "I love both the French Canadians and the Irish because I have the blood of both in my veins, but I cannot help comparing the Irish and the French who have worked in the mills. It has taken the French Canadian three generations to get out and achieve what the Irishman did in one; namely, build himself a nice home, plan a good education for his children, and strive to better himself in his work."

A fact which makes for slow progress on the part of the French Canadians, and which is frequently forgotten, is that they are the newest immigrant group. Every other group has been able to rise on the shoulders of a still newer group, but this has not been possible for the French Canadians, who have been able to use in this fashion only their own people who have come in successive waves to take jobs at the lower rungs of the ladder. In addition, their continuous migration to the mills and factories has blurred the picture of the progress of the group as a whole. Some of them have made the self-same advances as have been made by members of other groups, but the rate of advance on the whole seems more halting and slow.

Within the German and the Italian groups differentiation of labor is less obvious. The Germans have always been held in high respect as workmen in whatever occupations they were engaged. In the early days many of them worked as weavers in the mills, or in the lumber yards; now they are skilled artisans, able contractors and builders, and business men. Their advance in the professions has been marked. Of fifty-seven first- and second-generation German householders, none of the twenty-seven members of the first generation was in the professions, while three of the thirty members of the second are so listed. The Italians are too few in number and have been here too short a time to show the same shift in occupations exhibited by the longer established groups, but the same general tendency to move from unskilled to skilled occupations is evident. One half of fifty-five first- and second-generation householders are in the manufacturing and mechanical industries or in transportation. With one or two exceptions, however, they do not work in the cotton mill, the domain of the French Canadians, but instead are laborers in the factories, truck drivers, and workers on the railroads; a few even have independent manufacturing establishments. One seventh of the Italians are in trade, having either independent groceries or fruit stores; two, or 4 per cent, are in the professions.

In relation to the position of the majority of their members, two ethnic groups — the Yankees and the French Canadians — stand in the main at opposite ends of the economic ladder. Their place in the economic life of the city forms the design of two inverted triangles; the French-Canadian triangle rests upon the broad base of 75 per cent of the householders as laborers and rises to the point at the top where 2 per cent are in the professions, while the Old American triangle roughly presents the reverse picture — the broadest base being in the professions and white-collar occupations of the community, and the apex in a small representation among the unskilled laborers. The other ethnic groups fill in the remainder of the design.

The stability of this design inevitably breeds attitudes of superiority and inferiority as a majority of one group remains at one or the other end of the economic scale; and furthermore, it tends to encourage subtle prejudices and discriminations as the newer groups advance. Whether such prejudices, for the most part unconscious, originate in industry or are a reflection of prejudices prevalent throughout the community, the effects are the same: economically, to prevent the individual from being judged on his own merit in seeking a job; socially, to hinder the free intercourse which would otherwise be natural between persons with common occupational interests and economic concerns.

These prejudices and preferences have always existed in American industry. As Herman Feldman has pointed out in *Racial Factors in American Industry*,[1] they range from mild preference for one group to marked discrimination against another. Under many circumstances they produce grave injustices. In Burlington, however, these prejudicial attitudes are not at work in the same way that they are in large industrial centers. They are modified somewhat by the fact that in such a small community the general impression of the group can be offset by personal acquaintanceship with an individual who has risen from the ranks. Of course, the subtle loyalties which affect the actions of a member of a group still exercise their force. An Old American woman, for example, explained that

[1] New York: Harper & Brothers, 1931.

she would unthinkingly choose an Old American doctor rather than an Irish doctor just because the Old American was " one of our people." Only in part are such loyalties offset by the traditional American admiration for the poor boy who has succeeded. The community takes a certain pride in its Irish doctors, even in its Jewish lawyers, as they are proofs that America is still the land of equal opportunity for all, but their competition with Old Americans is on a slightly different basis from that of other Old Americans.

Generalization in regard to a group is still a pervasive tendency, among the older elements being expressed in its mildest form by showing a marked preference for the English or the English Canadians as being people "like ourselves." In the minds of many citizens the Greeks, Syrians, and Italians are lumped together as a very doubtful element, with question in the minds of some as to whether even to consider them as "white." Concerning the Italians specifically, the suspicion dies hard that "they are not to be trusted; they might stick a knife in your back." The extent to which such prejudices live on nothing is indicated by the fact that this impression of the Italians persists in the face of evidence that in Burlington they have an unusually clean court record. In addition, people of the same working class are distrustful of each other. The French Canadian does not like the Italian, the Italian distrusts the Greek, the Greek is suspicious of the Jew. All of these emotions cut through the common concerns of the working class itself.

The group which suffers most under the general feeling of inferiority is the French-Canadian. Dismissed by the Old American with the one word "static" — "They are just where they were twenty-five years ago" — they are not sure of themselves. As one French Canadian explained: "A French Canadian is always afraid that he won't be able to do his job well enough. He has to have ten times the amount of knowledge of it that an Irishman has before he will go ahead. Then he is thorough, careful, and conscientious. The Irishman with one tenth of the knowledge will get along on bluff."

Differences of opinion among employers in regard to the French Canadians are marked. On the one hand, one employer of some one hundred French Canadians said: "I never saw a more hard-working group of people. They are willing to work long for very little pay, and they are as thrifty as any Yankee." On the other hand, the foreman in another factory explained: "The French are just happy, easy-going; they are glad to earn enough for today and don't worry much about tomorrow. They never think of getting a better job. They take it for granted that they are going to do this kind of laboring work all the time." A banker justified his unfavorable estimate of the race with the explanation that "they intermarried with Indians in early days and so became irresponsible." And a woman, seeking a maid, translated one unfortunate incident in which a French-Canadian girl had stolen from her into a general disinclination to hire any more French Canadians: "You can't really trust them." These judgments, whatever the experience or lack of it that prompted them, influence the employers in determining the type of work for which they feel the French Canadians qualify; and their attitudes in regard to the group tend to be reflected throughout the community.

Religion and language sometimes play a part in determining the selection of a French Canadian for a position. In some Protestant concerns he may be rejected on the ground that he will disturb the necessary balance between Catholic and Protestant employees. In regard to the language handicap, some young salesmen of French-Canadian descent have felt that in spite of their college training they have not been as successful as they might be with prospective customers partly, at least, because of their French accent, which has called forth such remarks as "I do not care to buy anything from a foreigner."

No other group, however, lives under the same complex of prejudicial attitudes as the Jews, even in Burlington. It is a plexus of prejudices centuries old in which economic rivalry, religious differences, and objection to unpleasant individual characteristics are interwoven; the very complexity of these prejudices makes them all the more difficult to eradicate. All Jews suffer from them, but those who feel them most are those who have to seek employment among the peoples of other races and religions. Since in Burlington these prejudices are so like those which the Jews have met everywhere in the world, it would be useless to attempt within the framework of this study to add anything to an understanding of this specific problem, which deserves to have, and has had, many complete volumes devoted to its consideration. The varying forms which prejudice takes in Burlington are therefore merely outlined here.

One form of prejudice against the Jews in business is based largely on jealousy of their economic advance. As many people have pointed out: "You never see a Jew as a laborer or a Jewish girl as a maid. They won't take these jobs. They are only interested in getting the best white collar jobs and getting into the professions. If they were only willing to do the others too, we wouldn't mind their aiming for the top." Another illustration of the form which this prejudice takes is seen in the remark made by one business man in Burlington who explained: "No, I don't employ any Jewish help. I did once, though. He was a fine worker and brought in a lot of business; but as soon as he had learned the trade he started a shop of his own. I wouldn't employ another Jewish clerk. I don't want any more competition in my business."

The most frequent generalization directed against the Jews in Burlington, as elsewhere, is that they are loud and aggressive. The difficulty of changing this generalization to an attitude based on individual experience is indicated by the remark of another business man who said: "I know there are some fine Jews, but I don't let myself get to know them too intimately. If I did, I would find the usual Jewish characteristics that I so dislike."

This persistent seeking of undesirable characteristics will, of course, always discover them. By such a process a man closes the door of his mind and retires behind it to cherish his preconceptions.

On a lower level are the remarks so frequently heard in Burlington, ranging from the definite rejection by some customers of certain stores — "They look Jewish, the way they pile their goods on the counter; you'd think you were buying from a peddler's cart" — to the superstitious awe expressed by one old Frenchman: "Sure, I always buy my groceries in a Jewish store. You get good buys. And haven't you noticed that a Jew is successful where other people fail? There's something to it that they are God's Chosen People." An interesting commentary on the bases of such prejudicial attitudes is provided by the story of what happened to one woman who went into a Burlington store and selected a clerk to wait on her.

"I picked you out to wait on me," she explained, "because I didn't want to be waited on by a Jewish girl."

"Oh," said the Jewish girl, "didn't you know that this is a Jewish store?"

Yet the pride which such a community as Burlington feels in its own world as distinct from the world outside serves to mitigate the prejudice against the Jews within the city to some extent. The community feels a certain loyalty to its Jews. They are known as individuals; their business standards are not so unlike those of others as might have been supposed. Many business men point out: "The Jews here are different; they are not like the Jews in New York who try to grab everything and make money on you at every turn. These are fine people here in Burlington. Of course I don't know them well, but they are a good class of Jews." At the same time, many Jewish business men along Church Street explain that, though at first they were looked at askance and with reserve, this attitude on the part of the other business men gradually broke down as the likeness of interests was discovered.

Many gestures of appreciation and understanding offset the innumerable prejudices separating the ethnic groups. There is in Burlington a very real effort on the part of employers and employees to cut through their first prejudices to a more just evaluation of the individual. Certainly there are cases to prove that the first suspicious attitude towards a business neighbor of a foreign group has altered to respect. Furthermore, many business men have learned that it is good business policy to disregard whatever prejudicial feelings they may have. The department stores have found that it pays to have representatives of each religious group and of each large ethnic group as employees. Recognition of the size of the French-Canadian group and its purchasing power has resulted in the policy of having on each floor at least one clerk who can speak French. Even some banks — the organizations considered most highly selective in their choice of employees — have gone so far as to employ one or two Catholics. Whatever the reason for these gestures, the fact remains that they are being made; and they may ultimately lead to a truer understanding of the qualities to be found in every group. A prejudice must be deeply rooted to withstand the force of experience.

These, however, are but the first halting steps in a new

direction. Throughout the community the picture of racial coöperation and appreciation in the business world still leaves much to be desired. In Burlington there is still one bank which does not employ a Catholic. None of them employ Jews. Only one of the non-Jewish chain stores on Church Street has any Jewish help. All these facts help to make the Catholics and Jews feel that they are being discriminated against, and whether the prejudices are real or imagined matters very little. The effect is the same; they erect barriers in the economic life of the city, and these project into every aspect of community relations. Until prejudicial attitudes are dissipated, and individualization takes the place of generalization, these barriers will continue to block the free intercourse which provides the only possibility for a realization of the potentialities of all members of the community.

It may well be, of course, that such attitudes will not be dissipated by any conscious effort; such efforts often emphasize the differences they would eradicate. But other forces are at work, other interests are springing up to supersede interest in ethnic differences. Particularly since the economic and political uncertainty of recent years, consciousness of class is coming to be more important than consciousness of "race" as such.

The principal breakdown of ethnic distinctions has been occurring on the middle level of Burlington's economic life. As an Irish Catholic business man explained: "There isn't any racial or religious prejudice among the business men of Church Street any more. There is a nice friendly atmosphere. Sure, the matter of religion has come up sometimes in certain community activities, but not in business. I think that religious prejudices are only left in odd corners of Burlington, where people haven't anything much more to think about and so they build up a lot of imagination about the other fellows. I face the world with good feeling for my fellow man and I personally don't meet any religious prejudice."

Another Catholic business man expressed himself in the same way: "When I began to work for a Protestant firm on Church Street, I was a curiosity. They didn't know what kind of a person a Catholic was. When in addition they learned that I voted Democrat rather than Republican, they were pretty upset for a while. The manager came and warned me that I wouldn't get anywhere by voting the Democratic ticket. But I told him there were two things that he couldn't advise me on, my religion and my politics. If they were offensive to him, he could fire me."

Such an attitude indicates that in their pursuit of profits the Burlington business men would not let racial or religious distinctions interfere, and also that they would enter into alliances which would be of mutual assistance.

A significant institution which helps to maintain unanimity of action and spirit in the business men's world and which cuts across ethnic and religious lines is the Chamber of Commerce. Not only do most of the business men on Church Street belong, but the Chamber is trying to get the shopkeepers on North Street to join. Within the organization there have been several recent examples of united action involving business men of many ethnic and religious groups, including a number of prosperity drives, when the papers were filled with advertisements of bargains offered by all the merchants. In addition, the business men of Burlington share a faith in the traditional American belief that "any man can get ahead if he just gets the breaks." This has not been seriously affected by the depression, although there is a general feeling that the possibility of getting ahead may be hurt by further governmental interference in business. An indication of the nature of this belief is afforded by the words of one Catholic business man: "Oh, yes," he explained, "there's still lots of opportunity to work your way to the top. As a matter of fact, it is easier than it used to be in Burlington. At least racial and religious distinctions aren't so important."

Among the workers at the lower level of Burlington's economic life, this optimism is not so general. It is expressed in a different form. As one French Canadian who had lost his job said: "Yes, I think things will be better for us than they are now. But I don't hope for the things I used to believe I could have. Things will improve, but not for our generation. Maybe for our children." The old faith in getting ahead seems to be going down as a motivating force and no new one has developed to the point where it can act as a unifying ideal. The realization, as one Irishman said, that "there's damn little fat in thinking you're better than an Eyetalian if neither of you can pay the rent" has not produced an alignment of workers comparable to that afforded the business men by the Chamber of Commerce. Still, some importance must be attached to the fact that beneath the pressures of economic disorder the French-Canadian mill worker, the Italian truck driver, and the Irish clerk in one of the department stores are thinking in similar terms and striving for one thing — security. The French-Canadian wife of a factory worker said: "The important thing is for John to get a job. I don't care what kind, so long as we would be sure of a roof over our heads and three meals a day." A German woman, wife of a skilled laborer, said: "What does it amount to to get seventy-five cents an hour anyway? It looks like big pay at the time, but Paul has steady work only from April to October, and the rest of the time we wonder if we are going to get through the winter. I'm keeping my eye out for a job where a couple can get a cottage and keep for taking care of some home or institution. It isn't what we once hoped for, but at least we'd be sure of steady work." An Italian wife said: "What can you do with eighteen dollars a week and four babies to feed and clothe? And during slack time Angelo doesn't work at all. The other night he said to me, 'I will stay home with the kids and you go to the movies.' But I said, 'Twenty-five cents! I can buy a pair of pants for Joey with that, and he sure needs them.' Say, if the boss would only give Angelo even twenty dollars a week, we would buy more things in the grocery stores. That would help business and we'd all do better."

Only a few persons go beyond these troubled reflections to express a more definite feeling that their worries are the worries of a class to which another class "on the hill" is in opposition. One woman, for example, said: "The trouble with Burlington is that there aren't more industries in town. If there were, the working people could get together more and ask for better wages. But the people on the hill didn't want any factories. They said they didn't want the blue sky spoiled by smoke. And so they have their blue sky and we eat grass."

The need for economic security is a common concern of the working class even as the desire for profit is common to the business men. They are all troubled by the lack of such security. Yet, as can be seen, they advance no solution and only rarely do they place any blame. They are thinking alike, but they are not thinking together to any great extent.

Unions, the one possible institution which might cut across the ethnic barriers that separate the members of the working class as the Chamber of Commerce has for the business class, do not flourish in Burlington. Formerly they were active in the town; there was even a central Building Trades Council. It is said that it was this organized group of seven hundred laborers who, with their families and friends, at one time determined the election of Mayor Burke, the first Irish mayor of Burlington. But after the war unions began to mean less and less, and during the depression they almost wholly disappeared.

Today, however, the eight that still exist are a little more hopeful. As one of the men in the Carpenters' Union explained, "The membership sank from 212 to ninety during the depression, but it is now back to 106 members. They still meet once a week, but the meetings aren't social functions any more." Those who are members are convinced that their organization is a bulwark against the employers' desire to lower the wages of skilled workmen. The community as a whole, however, whether employee or employer, gives little support to the unions. As one Yankee workman explained, "The whole trouble with the working class is that they don't yet know what it is to hang together."

In the face of the general apathy of the working-class group and the conservatism of the other groups in the community, any trust in a working-class movement is slow in developing among workers of the city. Loyalty to a religious or ethnic group and the still-pervasive belief in individual opportunity are powerful forces in preserving the *status quo* and counterbalancing any such movement. Even when some degree of coöperation is achieved, the community knows little about it, since its newspapers evince a general disinterest in organized labor. On June 5, 1934 a strike began in the cotton mill in Burlington, and not until June 12 was any comment on it made in the newspapers. At that time a short column on the ninth page was headed "Labor dispute not yet settled." On June 18 another brief comment was added: "Trouble is not 'mere nonsense'! This was the answer of the union organizer to the verdict of a Burlington judge that the whole trouble down at the cotton mills was foolish nonsense." On June 27 the strike was deplored because it put 280 people on the charity list at a time when the city should have lower expenses; the following day it gained an editorial on "Expensive Facts." Long before the strike was settled, the mayor spoke with the men and assured them that they wouldn't lose by going back to work while the matter was being settled in Washington. To this plea he added the threat that, since the company was ready to assume operations, the strikers could expect no more relief from the city. These things had their effect; the workers returned, and Burlington breathed a sigh of relief.

The history of this strike had a twofold effect on the workers. For some it strengthened militancy through recognition of the strength and nature of the opposition; these, a small number, have remained with the union. As one of them commented: "My friends have warned me that if I stick by the union I will have to eat a lot of crusts, but I am willing to do so. I believe it is the only way a working man can get justice. And believe me, maybe only a handful of fellows now pay their dues; but I bet that if it came to a showdown, 51 per cent of the mill are at heart in favor of the union. The company didn't win that strike. We did. We learned our strength without hurting ourselves by staying out too long."

For others, however, the defeat of the strike spelled a disillusionment that will be hard to overcome. As one worker remarked: "Belonging to a union means strikes. That means you go without your pay checks. And that means you get in debt and it takes weeks to get out. I didn't think that's what it would mean to join the union. I thought we would get things by arbitration. It's no use bucking the company about a foreman who hasn't treated the girls right or about a stretch-out policy. The company will get their own way until somebody bigger than they are can stop them."

Thus, although there is a growing realization, if not of positive unity, at least of a unity in opposition to another class, the movement that might unite all workers of whatever ethnic or religious background proceeds in zig-zag fashion, receiving almost as many checks as it does pushes. The building of high hopes upon the textile strike did, it is true, affect employer-employee relations at Lakeside. It also, however, split the workers into two groups — one still trusting in the union, the other opposed to it. Friendships were broken, and the community spirit was jarred. Each side is convinced that the other is wrong, and each gets comfort in his point of view from his pastor. As one workman goodhumoredly explained, "When Father Plomandon says from the pulpit, 'In union there is strength,' one side thinks he is referring to the textile union. The other says it is the Union of St. Jean Baptiste."

The church is a strong power in preventing any class alignment among the workers. This is particularly true of the Roman Catholic Church, which numbers among its followers the largest percentage of working people. One French Canadian said: "Apparently the Lord doesn't want us to have the happiness of having steady work. He most likely feels that if things were too easy for us we would forget Him. I don't think we would forget Him, but I suppose He knows best." Sermons are preached on the importance of the worker's respecting the authority of the employer; although, as one priest said, "Both employer and employee should be governed by Christ's teachings." Class conflict, it is pointed out, means a denial of Christ.

It is doubtful, however, if the opposition needs to be on quite this level. The workers as a whole, though troubled, are far from revolutionary. There are no Communists among them. There is a little radical talk, but this is generally dismissed as mere "drug-store talk; it doesn't mean that anything will be done." The most revolutionary remarks made by the workers are unconsciously so. A Frenchman in the woolen mills, for example, said: "When the government stepped in and set up relief agencies and promised to help the poor, it saved this country from revolution. But then again, if there hadn't been any relief, the people might have gotten together sooner and gotten what they really wanted, more than they now have."

These, then, are some of the thoughts that are surging through the minds of even the docile workers of Burlington. Although still vague, they are at the moment more important than questions of ethnic or religious distinction, which they may in time supersede.

CHAPTER VI

HOW THE KINGDOM OF GOD DIVIDES
AN AMERICAN CITY

IN BURLINGTON, Sunday is still a day for going to church. Throughout the morning people are to be seen walking quietly along under the Gothic arches of elms in the direction of the churches. In the Sabbath stillness the old Puritan traditions seem to reassert themselves. For a moment one may believe that on this day the differences and cleavages fall away and all men bow humbly before the sense of a common destiny of mankind, as expressed in the Fatherhood of God and the Brotherhood of Man.

Such a reverie, however, is soon broken. The jangling of church bells reminds one that many congregations and sects are calling to their faithful to come and worship in the true way, the only way to gain the Kingdom of God. There are eleven divisions within the Protestant faith, three within the Catholic, and three within the Jewish. Before the divisive forces of sect and creed the great unifying power of religion seems as naught.

The theological reasons for so many churches for Burlington's 25,000 people lie buried in ecclesiastical history. They have small importance today. Only the three major divisions into Catholic, Protestant, and Jewish still retain a philosophical justification. The original issues which determined men to select one sect or another have more or less been replaced by social or economic distinctions.

Among the Protestant churches, one is now a democratic church, appealing mostly to the working class, another appeals to the successful business class, and a third to the professors. The three synagogues among the Jews grew up solely because of personal differences within an orthodox group. Similarly, the three Catholic churches express differences other than those of belief. One church ministers primarily to the needs of the Irish, the other two to the needs of the French Canadians.

The Catholic Church still commands the greatest interest on the part of its members. The two main Catholic churches, Irish and French-Canadian, for example, hold six Masses every Sunday and at each Mass the churches are filled. In sharp contrast, a handful of Protestants may be seen entering their churches at eleven o'clock for their one service. At the largest synagogue there are usually between fifty and sixty persons in attendance Friday night, though on special holidays the attendance is swelled to two or three hundred. Many explanations have been brought forth to account for the discrepancy in church attendance between the Catholics and the Protestants, in the light of the similarity of beliefs held by the average member of each church. Some Catholics say that the Protestants aren't religious; while some Protestants, on the other hand, criticize the Catholics for subservience to the forms of religion. The real explanation, however, seems to be the difference in authority. One French-Canadian Catholic said: "I go to church because we are taught that if we don't go we are lost. The main objective in life is to get to heaven and without going to church we can't get there." A Protestant, on the other hand, remarked: "Of course I don't always go to church myself, but I do feel we should support the church. It is the institution our fathers established, and it means a good deal to a lot of people. I don't know what would happen to the country if we didn't have churches." There is no question here of a difference in subservience to form, the difference is in the imperatives: one is religious, one is social; one is weighted with authority, the other is not.

This question of authority is the one principle upon which Catholics and Protestants may be said to be divided as religious groups. Both, it is true, believe in authority; but for each it rests upon a different base. To the Catholics, authority is invested in the Church which was established by God to interpret His word and guide His people. To the Protestants, on the other hand, authority rests in the Bible; and they are permitted a limited degree of freedom in interpreting the Word. This division is more than merely a difference in religious belief. It involves two totally different philosophies of living, and conditions actions that extend far beyond the realm of the spiritual.

Today two opposed tendencies may be seen in the Protestant Church in Burlington as in the rest of the world — one working toward an intensification of the difference between Catholic and Protestant conceptions, one working toward a lessening of the difference. In the growth of humanism can be seen a further development away from authoritarianism. As one minister explained: "Yes, I believe that there will be a religious revival, but it will be the religion of man's faith in himself. This is the first time a major depression has failed to bring people back to the Church, and I think that's a good thing. I think it is a mark of maturity of man that he doesn't feel that it is God being angry with him or that He had anything to do with it. It is part of man's high heritage to bear the brunt alone, and as he will be able to do this he will gain a great sense of spiritual strength and freedom."

Opposed to this movement away from authority in religion is a tendency which expresses itself in the stand taken by another clergyman in the community. "What is necessary," he said, "is a return to religious discipline. I do not mean we should go back as far as fundamentalism, but the Church must regain its authority." This movement, if it should gain in force, would bring the Protestants closer in philosophy to the Catholics. It would put the minister in a position comparable to that of the priest, except that, as one clergyman explained, "where the priest is clothed in the ecclesiastical authority of an organization, the minister would be clothed in the authority of the Word." One expression of this tendency is the Oxford Group movement, which recently held its first large meeting in Burlington. Yet with all these movements and changes the man in the street is only slightly concerned in his everyday life; to the great majority of Burlingtonians religion is a Sunday matter which gets its proper consideration on that day and only under special circumstances is thought about on other days.

That a general lack of concern with religious beliefs as

such should exist in a community where religious affiliation is a matter of great importance is an anomaly that demands explanation, for certainly a religious cleavage does exist in the community. Other differences pale into insignificance beside it; ethnic and social struggle is contained in it; every person, whether he wishes it or not, is made conscious of his religious affiliation. One indication of this is in the reply of a six-year-old boy who, when asked what his nationality was, answered, "I am a Catholic." The effort was made to clarify the question by asking, "Yes, but what is your nationality? Are you French, German, or Irish?" His answer was doggedly the same: "I am a Catholic." Even adults throughout the city, when asked their nationality, frequently answered by stating their religion. Obviously this religious affiliation signifies something far more important to them than their differences in religious belief would indicate. What is it?

The deepest roots of religion are social rather than theological. As Herbert Adolphus Miller points out:

> Religion is always organized socially. From the heathen, who, in his blindness, bows down to wood and stone, to the most complex ecclesiastical systems, man has worshipped his divinities in associations the basis of which has not been theological harmony, but rather some prior grouping, not essentially religious. In other words, a religious system is originally secondary to the group in which it is found. It may develop such power as to have actual priority in consciousness; but even where this seems to be the case, conflict inevitably reëstablishes the original relationship in which the group takes precedence over the religion.[1]

---

[1] *Races, Nations and Classes* (Philadelphia: J. B. Lippincott Company, 1924), p. 39.

Frequently the social need which religious organization answers is that of expressing the integrity of a group and its independence from another. This is especially true when a condition of oppression exists.

"In the hands of a national group dominated by another, religious institutions become most powerful means of defense both as organizations and symbols of solidarity." [1] Over and over again minority groups in Europe have found religion a tool for just such a use. The Jews are perhaps the outstanding example of this. Their identity has been preserved through the symbol of their religion although they have been scattered among the peoples of the earth. It has even been said of the Irish that, had the English been Roman Catholic, they would have been ardent Protestants in order to maintain their identity and assert their differences from the English.

In Burlington, too, the religious issues conceal a greater social struggle. Here in New England, the home of Protestant democracy, the struggle is of Old Americans striving to protect their Puritan conception of America against the invasion of elements not only foreign but Roman Catholic, not only of an alien tradition but imbued with a philosophy fundamentally opposed to Protestantism. On the other hand, the Catholic camp represents in part the organization of the newer elements into an assertive alliance that also serves as a protection against the dominance of the older elements. In every social situation, one

[1] *Ibid.*, p. 40.

way of stating this struggle is in terms of two questions:
What new ground have the Catholics gained? Are the
Protestants holding their own? Before this struggle for
community priority, the Jewish question is of minor importance. The Jews are a small group, considered alien
by each of the others and only called upon by each in
community situations where it is felt that they will aid in
the major conflict.

At first glance this conflict of old elements and new
elements under the opposed banners of Catholicism and
Protestantism would seem to have little to do with the
question of ethnic differences. Yet, insofar as each camp
represents the alliance of diverse ethnic groups for whatever reason, it is a factor in the amalgamation of those
groups. Such an alliance shows for each group its recognition of an identification with a larger unit than that of
its own people.

This identification is not complete, however. Within the
Catholic Church — the Mother Church of most of the
immigrant groups in Burlington — there has been since
earliest times a division between the French Canadians
and the Irish. Although both are members of the same
faith, they have never, except perhaps in the earliest days
of the settlement, worshipped together. Always the French
Canadians have insisted on a church to serve their own
people as distinct from any other. In 1850, notwithstand-
ing the friendly gestures toward coöperation, and the opposition to separation on the part of the Irish, they obtained
official sanction for the establishment of a nationality

parish — the first French-Canadian parish in the United States. From that day onward, through the untiring efforts of Bishop DeGoesbriand, the French parish was strengthened by the arrival of missionaries from Brittany and Canada.

The reason usually given for the rift is that the French are unable to fulfill their religious obligations in any other than their native tongue. "Why else," said the priest of St. Anthony's parish, "did the apostles receive the gift of tongues before they went out to teach the people, if there was no realization that each person must worship in his own tongue?" Yet this explanation of the need for separatism is only partially valid, for when it is no longer necessary to preach to a congregation in the tongue of its fathers, there is still a desire to keep the congregation separate. Today, recognizing that more and more of his people now speak English, the French priest of St. Joseph's parish gives one Mass every Sunday — the Children's Mass — in English. Thus while language difference is an excuse for separatism, it is not the reason for it; the real desire is to maintain ethnic identity, of which language is one expression. Religion is the first front on which an ethnic group asserts its difference from the Old Americans; language is the second, on which it would assert its difference from those of the same religion, and that second front is beginning to break down.

Today, although the early division of parishes on this basis still exists, it is growing less easy to maintain. Many of the French Canadians, particularly those of the younger generation, are finding a community of interest with others of their religion. They speak the same language, may work in the same stores, live on the same street. They see no reason why they should not worship together. More and more they are becoming members of Cathedral Parish.

This movement both Irish and French watch with some concern. The Irish of the congregation are not enthusiastic over the large influx of French Canadians and feel that since the French Canadians have a nationality parish, they should remain loyal to it and give it their much needed support. The Irish interpret much of the French-Canadian migration to Cathedral Parish as a result of the tardiness of the French church in adapting its services to the large number of its congregation who understand only English. They also feel that for many French Canadians to join the Cathedral Parish symbolizes a rise in social status.

Keen as is the concern of the Irish with the growing French-Canadian membership in the Irish parish, it does not compare with the concern of the French-Canadian leaders who believe, as Bishop DeGoesbriand did, in the nationality parish. To them this movement is but one more indication that they are being absorbed in the larger parish. As they point out, they have had to make concessions to the more powerful Irish; they have had to accept the leadership of an Irish bishop, even Irish leadership in the religious orders connected with the entire parish, some of which were not only originally French in leadership but were also French in language and spirit, and now they watch with growing alarm this increasing movement of French Canadians into the Irish parish. This movement, the French Canadians are convinced, the leaders of the Irish parish do nothing to discourage; in fact, in the French Canadians' view, they encourage it. It is, for example, a rule that any boy who wishes to attend the one parochial high school, connected with the Cathedral Parish, must pay tuition unless he is a member of that parish, and no girl may attend unless she is a member of the parish. This is a powerful persuasive to those French Canadians who wish their children to have a high school education under the parochial school system and who cannot afford to pay tuition.

The situation described indicates three things: first, how under social pressure the minority groups combine to present a united front; second, how behind that front they split because of the effort of each group to maintain its ethnic integrity; third, how before the cohesive forces of sharing a common religion, living in the same world, speaking finally the same language, the barriers set up between the ethnic groups by this desire to maintain ethnic identity are beginning to break down. Insofar as this breaking down of barriers behind the front of the Church implies a recognition of common ties within the Church, religion may be said to be, in part, accomplishing the task of Americanization.

Yet when we have said that, we have said very nearly all, for with every breaking down of the barriers within each camp there is some tightening of the lines on a purely religious basis. Catholics are still separated from Protestants; and the greater unity each achieves serves but to strengthen that separation. Americanization is being accomplished, but only within two separate camps. Instead of being divided into numerous units, each representing an ethnic group, the community is divided into two, each representing a religious grouping. And until the ties which cut across these religious differences are discovered, as those which cut across ethnic differences are being discovered, the possibility of building a united community is remote. There are many illustrations of the way in which these religious differences have affected activities throughout the community.

When the Y. W. C. A. organized a business girls' club in 1931 composed of Catholic, Protestant, and Jewish girls, the Catholic girls, who had at first shown keen interest, all withdrew within a month's time. It was suggested then that perhaps if the organization had not been under the auspices of the Y. W. C. A. it might have been more successful, yet when a few years earlier an effort was made to organize a girls' club on an obviously secular basis, it had failed in exactly the same manner because the Catholic girls withdrew. A similar instance of the frustration of a community endeavor because of religious difference occurred in connection with the Y. M. C. A. Community Center recently built. Catholics, Protestants, and Jews had looked forward to the creation of this center as a provision for the social and recreational needs of the whole community. A few weeks before its opening, however, the order was given in the Catholic churches that no Catholic should be a member of the Y. M. C. A. Community Center. As a result, only a few Catholics have signed up for membership. All the Catholics who had been asked to be members of the Board sent their regrets. When criticized for this by the Protestants, they pointed out that the center was not really a community center but was identified with a Protestant institution first and the community second. Would the Protestants, they asked, be willing to send their children to a community house established by the Knights of Columbus? At the moment, the Catholics are hoping that some time in the future they will be able to build a Knights of Columbus center, satisfying the same needs as the Community Center in relation to a specific group, the Catholics.

The failure of the Boy Scouts to bring together the two groups in the community is a little more difficult to explain, for the Boy Scout organization is secular in origin, and throughout the country is supported by people of every race and creed. But even a national official — a Catholic — could not persuade the bishop of this diocese to permit Catholics to participate in the organization either in troops comprised of Catholics, Protestants, and Jews, or by organizing separate Catholic scout troops. The general Catholic feeling has been that the Boy Scouts in Vermont have been too closely connected with the Protestant churches; ministers have their fingers in the pie, and their influence cannot help but disaffect any Catholic youth who comes in contact with them. Such a stand, made on religious grounds, naturally places an emphasis on religious difference which is hard to overcome when community coöperation is desired.

A further illustration of these religious differences in the social field is afforded by the situation in the women's club which still is the most democratic club in the community. The Athena Club was organized as a study and social group with the hope that it would bring together all the women of the community — Protestant, Catholic, Jewish — who had a desire to use their leisure time. In the beginning this hope seemed to be fulfilled. There was a satisfactory representation from each of these groups, but shortly after the World War Catholic members began to withdraw. Soon thereafter, a local chapter of the Catholic Daughters of America was organized, with interest focused primarily on social service for the Catholic group and on study along religious lines. Inevitably this has affected Catholic membership in the Athena Club, even though it still remains the most democratic women's club in town. Many Catholic women, compelled to choose between joining the Athena Club and the Catholic Daughters of America, naturally choose the latter as something which holds their first interest and loyalty.

The growth of the two large hospitals in the community affords another interesting indication of the way in which a community enterprise is split on a religious basis. One of the hospitals, the Mary Fletcher, established in 1879, is a private, non-profit institution serving all people of all classes and creeds from all parts of the State. Until 1924 there was in addition a small Roman Catholic hospital on the outskirts of the city, but in that year a large one, the Bishop DeGoesbriand, was built in the center of the city. The erection of this hospital, following as it did close upon the building of the parochial high school, seemed to many people to mark one more step in the tightening of the lines in the community according to affiliation with the Protestant or the Catholic faith.

The friction that has resulted is reflected most clearly when each hospital puts on its annual drive for funds. Though both hospitals care for a large number of charity patients of both faiths, and though both include Catholics, Protestants, and Jews on their staffs, there are many Protestants who will not contribute to the Catholic hospital, many Catholics who will not contribute to what they now think of as the Protestant hospital. On the other hand, there are also many who assist in collecting money for both hospitals and take part in social activities planned for the raising of funds for each of them. Yet the division reasserts itself in those upper levels where coöperation of a more immediate nature is possible. The number of Catholics on the Auxiliary of the Mary Fletcher Hospital has decreased so that at present there is only one. The Bishop DeGoesbriand Hospital has never been able to persuade a Protestant to be on its Hospital Aid. No Catholic is a member of the Board of Directors of the Mary Fletcher, no Protestant a member of the Board of Directors of the Bishop DeGoesbriand.

Even politics is not free from the dividing force of religion. The political parties are Republican and Democratic, but the alignment is religious as well as political. The fact that this is so seems to one man active in community politics unfortunate in that it impedes alignment that is expressive of politically, instead of religiously, differing points of view. The association of Catholics with the Democratic party, of Protestants with the Republican, is such that, whatever his political beliefs, in ordinary times at least, no Irish Catholic can join the Republican party, no Yankee Protestant the Democratic, without some feeling that he has cut himself off from his kind.

In such a manner does the thread of religious dissidence, woven through every kind of community endeavor, weaken the fabric of community life. Again and again the people of the community, disinclined to admit that organized religion is dividing instead of uniting them, undertake new enterprises with renewed hope that they will bring them together in spite of their religious differences; again and again they find that religious differences do not cease to exist merely because they are denied; and as each enterprise fails there arise out of the sense of that failure new resentments, the Protestant blaming the Catholic, the Catholic blaming the Protestant.

If we are to understand the degree to which it will be possible to achieve a community of spirit that shall transcend religious divisions, it is essential that we understand the real basis for religious division, the real fears that keep such groups as Catholics and Protestants apart. They are, on each side, twofold. The Protestant may like the Catho-

lic as an individual, but he sees him primarily as a representative of a religious organization with a directing authority
outside the United States, to which the individual owes
first allegiance. This subjection to a visible spiritual authority seems to many Protestants dangerous to American
principles, because in times of crises, insofar as this authority is temporal as well as spiritual, it may occasion a
split in the loyalties of the individual Catholic between the
needs of his community and the demands of his Church.
No assurance given by the Catholic that there is no division
of loyalties is wholly convincing to some Protestants. The
Catholics may well exclaim as one did: "When has there
ever been a crisis in which Catholics haven't been able to
decide their loyalties? In any war Catholics flock to the
colors in the same way as do Protestants. They fight against
people of their own faith, they die, or they collect the bonus
in exactly the same way." But a Protestant, unconvinced,
murmured, "I like many an individual Catholic. But every
time another Catholic advances, the shadow of Rome gets
thicker over the community."

In addition to this fear of the authoritarian element of
Roman Catholicism, the Protestant Old American is reluctant to see a newcomer advance into activities, social,
political, or economic, to which he feels he has a prior
claim. He dislikes an Irish mayor not only because of the
association with the Roman Catholic Church, but because
he is taking a job for which the Old American feels he is,
by his American heritage, better equipped.

Similarly the Catholic may see the Protestant as an

attractive, if heretical, individual; but, more importantly, he sees him as a participant in an advancing movement which is attacking the very foundations of the "true religion." As one Catholic said: "It isn't the Protestant Church we fear. The power of Protestants is not in their Church. It is in the institutions and philosophy which grew out of Protestantism, and which, by their materialistic emphasis, are driving the world toward destruction." In addition, the average Catholic, usually a newer American, sees the Protestant as a member of a socially privileged group, anxious to protect his position and to assert his social advantages. And so the Catholic newer American resists him in a way not very dissimilar to that in which he resisted the domination of similar groups in the "Old Country." It was that domination which he came here to escape, and he will fight with astounding vigor anything which he interprets as similar here.

The name Catholic or Protestant, therefore, calls up in each of the groups in the community a complex of emotions composed of these three things — differences in belief, fear of the advance of a religious organization, and fear of the power that the social group has or may have, and so long as the fear which the Catholic feels of the "Protestant" and which the Protestant feels of the "Catholic" is not broken down and its components recognized, the community will continue to align itself on two opposed religious fronts. The Protestant hospital will be answered by a Catholic hospital; the public school by the parochial school; a Y. M. C. A. center by talk of a Knights of Colum-

bus center. The result is eventual stalemate. No enterprise reaches the entire community.

Yet in considering the possibilities in such a community
as Burlington, it must be remembered that the very size
of the city may serve to accentuate differences which in
other communities go unnoticed or seem less important.
In a smaller community the smallness of the groups prevents the kind of conflict which occurs in Burlington,
where the groups are large and prosperous enough to set
up such separate institutions as schools and the like. In a
larger community such institutions exist side by side and
their differences seem unimportant in the light of the
larger issues and more impersonal attitudes that the purely
urban environment occasions.

In addition, it must be noted that at the present time
the sense of religious difference, even in Burlington, is
affecting markedly only certain aspects of people's behavior. In other aspects, the very fact that the people do
live in the same community, work side by side, have the
same pleasures, has served to push the sense of religious
difference into the background. If these ties are given the
opportunity to develop gradually as in the past, the people
of Burlington may increasingly discover that their religious
differences, which now stand in the way of coöperative
social enterprises, are not so important as larger common
concerns. But the conflict still exists, and the possibility
for a gradual adjustment may become more remote as
Burlington is affected by outside forces. In the face of rapid
social change, the sense of religious difference such as exists

in Burlington may become a powerful force for dividing a people and rendering them subject to a calculating minority. This has occurred in Europe. It may not occur in the United States, but certainly the seeds of such a dissension still exist.

CHAPTER VII

MOLDING FUTURE CITIZENS — THE ROLE OF THE SCHOOL

TO A country with definite principles of democracy, immigrants from every nation in the world have come, bringing a variety of conceptions, political, cultural, and economic, all of which have to be adjusted to each other and oriented to the ideals upon which America was founded. Faced with the problem of unifying these diverse hordes, we have turned to that most democratic of American institutions, the public school. There, it has been hoped, the children — and through them the parents — of all races and creeds would be imbued with common ideals and directed toward common goals of American citizenship.

In the average urban community, however, instead of a single unified public school system there are two school systems — one the established, community-supported, public school, and the other that of an ethnic or a religious group. In some communities these parochial schools minister to the needs of half the children, and thus the very rock upon which it was hoped a common citizenship was to be built is split.

Why has this split occurred? Why, in a country which offers free education to everyone within its borders, have some people declined the offer and insisted on building, often at the cost of great personal sacrifice, separate schools?

Two powerful forces have combined to produce this result. One is the Church, which, eager to hold its people and afraid of the subversive power of the public school, has emphasized the importance of parochial schooling. The other is the desire of the newer ethnic groups to maintain not only their religion but also other cultural elements which have been important to them. The people as well as the Church see a danger that in the public schools these values will be lost; and so they strive to perpetuate them, to give them immortality through their children and their children's children. This importance of the parochial school to the ethnic group has been brought out by Znani-ecki and Thomas in *The Polish Peasant in Europe and America*: —

Good or bad, the parochial school is a social product of the immigrant group and satisfies important needs of the latter. The most essential point is neither the religious character of the parochial school, nor even the fact that it serves to preserve in the young generation the language and cultural traditions of the old country; it is the function of the parochial school as a factor of the social unity of the immigrant colony and of its continuity through successive generations. . . . Whereas children who go to public school become completely estranged from their parents, if these are immigrants, the parish school, in spite of the fact that its program of studies is in many respects similar to that of the public school, in a large measure prevents this estrangement, not only because it makes the children acquainted with their parents' religion, language and national history but also because it inculcates respect for these traditional values and for the nation from which they came. Moreover the school is not only a common bond between all the members of the old generation but is also considered by the young generation as their own institution, thus fostering their interest in the affairs of the Polish-American colony. The parochial school is a necessary expression of the tendency of the immigrant community to self-preservation and self-development.[1]

To all groups, training in the religious teachings of their fathers is on the surface, however, the most important reason for establishing separate schools, though behind the well-worn banner of religion the desire of each ethnic group to perpetuate itself as a social entity as well as to perpetuate its faith has been seen everywhere in America. Thus, for example, in the Middle West, Germans and Scandinavians of the same Protestant communion, and in the East, Irishmen and French Canadians of the same Catholic creed, build separate schools for their children.

In Burlington one is daily reminded of the fact that there are two school systems. Early in the morning, again at noon, and finally in the middle of the afternoon, the streets of Burlington are filled for a brief time with school children. The faces of all have that likeness notable in any mass grouping of young America. Yet, looking more closely, one may note that they are not one mass but two. Many of the childern are wearing every kind of dress and coat, but others, especially among the girls, are wearing one style of dress — green, blue, or black. In some sections of the city few of these uniformed young people are to be seen, but in other sections they are everywhere. They are wearing the badge of difference — their identification with the school of their people, the parochial school. They are

[1] Reprinted from *The Polish Peasant in Europe and America* by W. I. Thomas and Florian Znaniecki, by permission of and special arrangement with Alfred A. Knopf, authorized publishers. Pages 50–51.

almost as numerous as the children attending the public school: of the 5,701 pupils registered in Burlington in 1935, 3,291 were enrolled in the public and 2,550 in the parochial schools.

From the very beginning, in Burlington as in other communities, those who placed their hope in the public schools as a means of building a united citizenry have watched with regret the segregation of the newer elements in the parochial schools. They have tried vainly to make the public schools meet the demands of these newer peoples by modifying their religious activity, which was ostensibly the objectionable feature. Formerly a passage from the Bible was read to the children in general assembly; when this was criticized by the Catholics and the Jews because a Protestant form of the Bible was used, it was suggested that a rabbi, a priest, and a minister meet separately with the children of their respective faiths. This proposal, however, occasioned general objections as providing an un-American division into groups. Finally, under pressure, especially from the Catholics, it was decided to omit any religious exercises from the public schools and leave religious instruction to the churches, but when this was done the public schools were charged with being irreligious, and the Catholics continued to withdraw their children as fast as they could build schools for them. This situation differs from that in other communities only in that there is a larger proportion of Catholics than is usual, and so the conflict is perhaps more intense.

FUTURE CITIZENS

A group of Burlington school children costumed for a pageant. Their faces show the diversity of ethnic origin.

The first parochial school in Burlington was built shortly after the middle of the nineteenth century; by 1874 the present building which houses the Cathedral elementary school was erected; in 1916 a parochial high school was built. Since that time the parochial school system has continued growing. St. Mary's Academy, for instance, built in 1885 as a private school for girls, has now been supplemented by Trinity College, while not far outside the city is St. Michael's College for boys. There is talk of building a new parochial school to meet the needs of the Catholic children who now live in the south end of town.

But if the old inhabitants were dismayed by the withdrawal of the newcomers from the public schools in the name of their religion, the Irish were no less disturbed when the French Canadians, for the sake of their language, showed themselves disinclined to combine in a general parochial school. As far back as 1854 the French Canadians had established a French-Canadian parochial school. In 1869 they built the Nazareth School in the most densely populated French-Canadian section of the town. In 1928, on the site of this old school, they built a modern building to meet the growing needs of the French-Canadian parish. Not, however, content with this, and concerned with the French-Canadian children in the south end of town, they built in 1933 another parochial school, in St. Anthony's parish. Even the erection of this school does not mark the end of the establishment of French-Canadian schools within the Catholic school system. The hope is expressed that before long they will have money enough to erect a high school of their own so that their children of high-school age will not be lost in the large Cathedral High School, which is primarily identified with the Irish.

Of such bricks is the wall that divides the children of the community constructed. But is the division to be permanent? Do the people of the community want it to continue? An answer to the second question was secured by rating on a scale the attitudes of members of each ethnic group.

As might be expected, there are marked differences of opinion. The Old Americans, at one extreme, feel for the most part that every child should attend the public schools. The Irish, at the other, generally consider that all Catholic children should attend parochial schools. The other ethnic groups usually take a more moderate view.

The differences between the various groups and the reasons for them are interesting. Sixty-six of ninety-nine Old Americans who expressed an opinion believed that all children should attend the public schools. The remaining thirty-three showed some appreciation of the Catholic point of view and favored parochial education to a certain degree for children of Roman Catholic faith. Ten felt that it should consist of no more than one or two years during the early elementary training in order that the children may learn the rudiments of their religion; ten would extend the period through grammar school; eleven were willing to let it extend through high school; and two were even willing that it should go all the way through college.

Even among the sixty-six who believed in entire public school education, an appreciation of the needs expressed by the Catholics is evident. "I think," said one man, "that from the Catholic point of view it is undoubtedly important that the educational life of their children should be in the atmosphere of their own religious teaching. But from the civic point of view, I believe that religious training should be confined to the churches, and that the training for citizenship should be paramount in the school." The majority, however, feel less sympathy with the Catholic rejection of the public schools: "I believe in a common school. Too strong an influence against Protestants is encouraged in the parochial schools." "In the training of children, why should such a decided line be drawn between Protestants, Catholics, and Jews? I believe in a public school under the domination of no one race or religion, where all can be trained in common traditions of citizenship. All schools should be under government supervision."

In marked contrast to the point of view of the Old Americans is that of the Irish. A solid front, seventy-four of the seventy-eight persons interviewed, took the stand that parochial education is necessary through high school; and over half of these would continue it through college. A burning conviction fortifies this stand: "If the parochial schools were closed today, this country would be a bedlam in less than twenty years." One first-generation Irishman went so far as to say: "If it were a choice between closing the church and the parochial school, the church should be closed first. It is the young people who must be influenced in the path of the right religion." Only four feel that parochial schooling need not extend further than one or two years, or at most through grammar school. Only one favored entire public school education.

Many commentators, however, have felt that the overwhelming emphasis placed by the Irish on parochial schools implies more than an interest in religion. The Irish, being leaders and spokesmen of all the immigrant Catholics, realize their power and are determined to lead the newer immigrant groups in an approach toward Americanism different from that of the Old Americans. This conception is not belied by the attitudes of the Italians and the French Canadians, who have considerably less power and are much less insistent on the need for parochial schools. Only 62 per cent of 141 French Canadians interviewed, as compared with 95 per cent of the Irish, feel that Catholic children should receive their entire education in the parochial schools; 25 per cent feel that parochial school education is necessary only through grammar school; 6 per cent, that a year or two of parochial school is enough; and 7 per cent, that no parochial education is necessary.

One reason for the comparative lack of interest in complete parochial schooling on the part of the French Canadians may be that they have no high school of their own. If they desire that their children be educated in a parochial high school, they must either pay tuition or identify themselves with the Irish by becoming members of the Cathedral parish. Some, however, finding it impossible to maintain their ethnic separation, are as willing to identify themselves with the public school as with the Irish parochial school. Another important reason for the French-Canadian attitude is that this group has a strong feeling of gratitude to the public schools because they teach French. Moreover, many do not contemplate sending their children much further than elementary school, and so are not concerned about high school or college. An attitude of simple faith activates some of the French — "We are supposed to go to parochial school; we have to obey if we are good Catholics." This is in strong contrast with the observation of another Frenchman who remarked: "The advantages of parochial or public school are a debatable question. I have observed in the business world that there are as many good Catholics among those who have come from the public schools as among those from parochial. It doesn't seem to make much difference to their religion."

Proportionally, the Italians show less concern than do the other Catholic ethnic groups as to whether or not their children attend parochial schools. Eight of thirty-eight Italians interviewed favored complete public education; six more felt that one or two years of parochial school are enough; eight thought that parochial education should extend only through the elementary grades; while only sixteen favored parochial education through high school, and less than half of these believed that it should continue also through college.

A reason frequently given for this small concern with

the question is that the public school is nearer the home, or that it is less expensive, or that the children should go to the best school whether it is parochial or public. The remarks of many Italians imply the desire to be identified with American culture. As one or another puts it: "I send my child to American public schools because she is now American and I want her to learn that. When she is older I will teach her to read and write Italian." Again, "The public school is cheaper and they get a good education there. I can teach religion at home."

The point of view of the Germans differs from that of either the Old Americans or the more dominantly Catholic ethnic groups. They are a small group, divided about equally between Catholics and Protestants. Seventeen of thirty-one persons questioned were in favor of public school education entirely. The other fourteen favored some parochial school education — two favoring it through college, seven through high school, four through grammar school, and one for a year or two.

The attitude of the Jewish group reflects an entirely different approach to the question of secular versus denominational education. As one man expressed the general feeling: "The American was wise in his realization of the place of the public school as a means of transition to American life. An American education is essential to the adjustment of our children to American life." Only eleven of fifty-seven persons interviewed favor a separate school for Jews, usually pointing out the Montreal system, with the three divisions in the Board of Education where Catholics, Protestants, and Jews each have separate schools. The remaining forty-six favor the public school system for all children. Thirty-nine of these, however, specified that they wished the children to attend the Hebrew Free School after regular public school hours in order that they might learn the religious traditions and language of their race.

Thus, in a representative selection from the community as a whole, only 25 per cent believe in a complete, all-inclusive public school system. Seventy-five per cent believe in the need for a parochial school system; but 15 per cent out of these 75 per cent believe that parochial education should function only a few years, 13 per cent believe in it through the elementary school, 20 per cent would carry it through high school, and 27 per cent want complete separation throughout educational life.

In addition, among the more ardent defenders of the parochial schools — the Irish and the French Canadians — it is notable that although from the second to the third generation there is a slight lessening of emphasis on the separation of their children throughout their *entire* education, they still want a greater proportion of parochial than of public schooling. There is practically no increase in the liking of the third generation over that of the second for complete or almost complete public schooling.

From all this it appears that the children of the community will continue to be divided into two groups — one exclusive, the other making an attempt to be inclusive and so to justify the hope placed in public education.

But do the people who want this division realize exactly what it means? The reason for this desire may be found in the interpretation of Znaniecki and Thomas, to the effect that "the parochial school is a necessary expression of the tendency of the immigrant community to self-preservation and self-development." It may be found in the words of the Catholic priest who said that "the child needs to be brought up in a day-long atmosphere of religion in order to learn the right way of life." Or it may be found in the words of the Protestant who said, "I don't think the Catholic realizes it, but I think the Catholic Church is manipulating his emotional needs in order to add to its own power. And the parochial school is the most potent expression of the Church's drive to maintain its power into the future." Each of these points of view undoubtedly contains part of the truth, but the important thing to note at this point is the method and result, whatever the motive.

Directly, the emphasis, particularly in the public school, is on breaking down any sense of difference between the students of the various ethnic and social groups. Activities are calculated to bring them together, and the whole stress upon standardization is designed to mitigate any sense of difference. Prejudicial attitudes, however, in the children, unconsciously acquired from their parents, and in the teachers themselves offset this influence to some extent. As the principal of one of the schools admitted, it is frequently difficult to remember to include the Jews in school activities. When they do take part, as in Burlington High

School where they are prominent in debating and cheer-leading, the results are doubtful. The other students tend to withdraw from debating, and there is a general feeling that some of the difficulty that at times is found in getting the school to cheer at games arises from an unwillingness to be led by Jews. In addition, once, at least, the question of teaching "The Merchant of Venice" caused the Jewish mothers some concern and for a time the play was left out of the course of study.

The parochial schools face no similar problem, since they have no Jews or Protestants in their classrooms. This fact, however, tends to make adjustment and appreciation even more difficult and thoughtless generalizations about a group easier. Recently a Sister in charge of a class reprimanded some girls before the class for wearing short socks. "Don't," she warned, "try to imitate the Protestants." In the minds of some of the students, at least, the implication was clear: Protestants are immodest, and probably immoral. Similarly many students became convinced that the Jews are a condemned race when a teacher in one of the classes told them that "the reason the Jews have been unsuccessful as farmers is because God wouldn't let things grow for them."

More important than these episodes, however, and sufficiently strong to offset any conscious attempt to overcome prejudicial attitudes, is the very fact that the community's children are separated on a religious basis. The way in which this separation works to foster a sense of difference and division may be seen in part from an analysis of the extent to which the two school systems are different and the extent to which they are alike.

Both school systems are the schools of many people. The public schools are, of course, a little more so than are the parochial in that they contain the ethnic groups that are Protestant and Jewish as well as those that are Catholic. In turn, the English-speaking parochial schools have a wider cross-section of the people than the French parochial schools. The children, whether they go to one school or another, go into classrooms that are much alike — low desks in rows facing a broad expanse of blackboard. On the blackboard there is frequently a motto or a quotation; but whereas in the public school this will stress civic or social virtues, in the parochial the emphasis will be on godliness. Similarly, though there are pictures on the walls of both schoolrooms, those in the public school are decorative or historical — "Washington Crossing the Delaware," "The Signers of the Declaration of Independence" — while those in the parochial school are religious — "The Last Supper," "Saint Theresa." A crucifix hanging on the wall also distinguishes the Catholic schoolroom. Both public and parochial schools, with one or two exceptions, have amazingly small playgrounds for their children.

The appearance of the teachers in the parochial schools differs from that of the teachers in the public schools. In the parochial schools they are either priests or nuns, although in one of the French-Canadian schools the nuns do not wear the conventional habit and therefore look more like public school teachers, and in the parochial high school one part-time teacher of dramatics is a Protestant. In the public schools there is no comparable uniformity in either appearance or faith. True, the largest proportion of the 104 teachers are Protestant, but it is estimated that eighteen of them are Catholic, and one is Jewish.

The qualifications of the teachers differ but little. For both public and parochial elementary schools, the teachers must be high school graduates and have had two years of normal school training; both must go to summer school periodically for further training. But while the teachers of the public schools go to summer session at the University of Vermont, the nuns go to the headquarters of their sisterhood, and a few do graduate work in Catholic universities. All attend state teachers' conventions. In recent years the same school nurse has served both schools. The same truant officer is called upon by both.

The foundation of the curricula is very similar in both school systems. All follow in a general way the outline of the state course of studies, though with independent choice of textbooks. There is, however, a definite difference in the textbooks that are presented to the two schools, in that one type is written from the Catholic point of view, the other from a secular, and each school feels that the texts of the other are biased, particularly in regard to the interpretation of history. The parochial schools spend a certain amount of time each day in specific Roman Catholic teachings, and in the French parochial schools in the teaching of French in addition. This is naturally not true of the public schools, except that French is taught in high school as a cultural language.

Methods of teaching differ from school to school, whether public or parochial, according to the teacher; but an analysis of the activity of one grade in each of these schools reveals those likenesses and differences which are ideological rather than idiosyncratic.

For the child going to Grade 1 in the elementary public school, the day begins with the salute to the flag. Then the day's work begins, to be interrupted once during the morning for a brief "recess" period. Throughout the day emphasis is put upon reading and what are called "Social Studies," designed to increase the child's understanding of social obligations and responsibilities. Through building a store, for example, he learns not only quantities, such as pints and quarts, and how to count and tell time, but also standards of honesty, of saving, and of wise spending. According to one of the teachers: "Throughout the year we strive to teach the child proper social habits; how to accept responsibility, how to be courteous. This is best realized through the English subjects and the social studies. Starting with responsibility in the classroom, they are taught responsibility in the home and then in larger fields, including the community and government."

The different emphasis in the parochial school is evident in the day's program. The Catholic child begins his school day with prayer, saying the "Our Father" and the "Hail Mary," then makes the same salute to the flag as the child in the public elementary school. After this, the usual classes of the day begin — reading, phonetics, music. The reading, as soon as it passes beyond the letter stage, has a religious emphasis; and the singing is often of hymns. Much of the time is spent in the first grade of parochial schools in learning the Catechism verbatim. In the child's education this Catechism study serves a purpose similar to that which the social studies serve in the public schools, although the emphasis is different. In the Catholic school the emphasis is upon learning and obeying the laws of God and preparing oneself for heaven; this, it is felt, will inevitably produce good citizenship. In the public school, the emphasis is upon learning basic social relationships in order that one may become a responsible member of society. In addition, the very technique of learning expresses the basic difference between the parochial and the public school way of thought: whereas in the public school the attempt is made through social studies to instill in the child a recognition of values achieved on the basis of experience, in the parochial school the habit is established of memorizing certain formulae which have been tested through the centuries. It is primarily on the question of which method will produce the better members of society that the parochial and the public schools remain divided.

This difference in emphasis carries right through the educational systems. While in the public school the social relations of modern society are being emphasized, in the parochial school the student is having stamped upon his

memory the teachings of the Church. The parochial
school day, but not the public school day, ends with a
prayer.

An additional difference serves to distinguish the day of
the student in the French-Canadian parochial schools from
the day of students in the other schools. In the small
elementary school that serves the newer French Canadians,
the first two hours of the morning are devoted to French,
or subjects in French, such as religion and the Catechism.
At the larger French-Canadian school, one hour is so devoted. This larger school places a greater emphasis on
discipline than the other schools: the children walk hushed
through the halls, do not speak while in line, and are
extremely obedient. Among the prizes distributed at the
end of the year are some for trying hard, and for citizenship. The latter prize, donated by the Daughters of the
American Revolution, is given to the child who, according to the principal, has shown the best sense of duty and
respect for authority.

Graduation from the elementary school has little meaning at either the Irish parochial or the public school, which
purposely attach little importance to this event, leaving
the child with the feeling that he is expected to continue
his education. Perhaps because of the smaller percentage
of its students that go on to high school, graduation from
the French-Canadian schools is a very important occasion.
The graduating class attends Mass and a Communion
Breakfast in the morning and receives its diplomas before
a large audience at night. A talk given by the priest em-

phasizes that they must remember their religious teachings; diplomas and prizes are given out; and the students present an entertainment program — consisting last year of folk dances and songs.

The High School in both school systems is a much more important world. Here standards of leadership become much more important. This leadership finds an outlet primarily in athletics. For an Irish boy the choice between going to Cathedral or Burlington High School is often based on the differences in the athletic opportunities in each. If he is really interested in getting to college by means of his athletic talents, he may stand a little better chance by going to Burlington High; this is especially true if he is interested in football, which is not played at Cathedral High.

In the high schools courses of study are the framework around which a complex social world is built. In both schools these are essentially a college preparatory course, a commercial course, and a general course. There is a certain choice of subjects in both. A junior in either school in college preparatory course will be studying English. In addition he may select subjects from a list including history, Latin, French, physics, mathematics. Those in the parochial schools will also be studying religion, while the girls in the public school may be studying home economics. An interesting reflection of the difference in emphasis placed by the two schools is to be found in the fact that whereas throughout the public school system the one subject compulsory in every grade is English, in the parochial school religion is similarly honored.

With this exception, the standards in both high schools are very similar, since they aim to meet either college requirements or the demands of business schools and business men, while both schools feel that they must somehow adapt themselves to meet the needs of an increasing body of students who by law are now required to continue in school even though they may be unable to meet the requirements of either the traditional college training course or the commercial course.

Surrounding these courses of study are a multitude of student activities, especially numerous in the public high school, where they are felt to be so important that school time is frequently given over to meetings. This emphasis on activity at Burlington High adds to the students' lives social distinctions more subtle than those found at Cathedral. In the public school the student organizations range from the Oread Board who publish the Yearbook, one of the highest educational honors, through the various language and music clubs, to the Dim-Wit Club, which in the lives of the public high school males apparently fills much the same place that a college fraternity does in the lives of their older brothers. In addition to these organized societies there are innumerable cliques and "crowds" which in general follow the social pattern of the children's parents, although belonging or not belonging to the "crowd" on which one has set one's heart is perhaps more important to the child than it is to the parent. The following conversation, overheard in the school halls, indicates the degree of group consciousness that can develop in the high-school child. A girl explained the desirability of going somewhere by saying, "All the best students are going." Her escort turned sharply and said, "What do you mean by 'best'? Those who get high marks or our crowd?" To "our crowd," to own a car or to be able to avail oneself of one on occasion to go to dances, and to have numerous dates, are of primary importance. These same values may not be shared by the rest of the school children, but they affect them. As many teachers explained, it is the people on the fringe of such a social unit who suffer, become self-conscious and unhappy. "If they could only realize," said one teacher, "that that group is not half as important as it thinks it is, nor as important as they think it is, these children would be much happier."

The social life of the parochial high school is much more simple in organization than is that of the public high school. Cathedral, with 334 students as compared with 1527 students in the public junior and senior high school, is a more personal school. Assemblies are not a weekly occurrence as in the public high school; and there is no time devoted within school hours either for club meetings or for orchestra or other music practice. The student organizations that do exist include some that are similar to those in the public high school. There is an orchestra, band, glee club, drama club. There is the editorial board of the Yearbook. Religious clubs tend to take the place of the clubs with a more social base that exist in the public high school. There are, for example, such religious societies as the Sodality of the Virgin Mary, the Mission units, and a Communion Club. There are also frequent "retreats" lasting usually for a week, during which Communion is taken daily and silent meditation is the order of the day. Dancing is not permitted in the parochial high school; dancing of any kind is not encouraged, and the one dance that does take place during the year is held outside the school. Even the annual class party takes the form of a banquet rather than of a dance as it does in the public school.

The two schools usually meet only on a competitive basis, either in games, at the annual musical festival, or when for a parade their two bands are called out. There is, however, a constant interchange of students. Sometimes pressure from the priest upon a child's family leads a student to change from the public to the parochial school, while on the other hand, the Catholic teachers occasionally encourage a backward or unruly child to transfer from the parochial school to the public school. These exchanges do not, however, bring the schools closer together, but in most cases merely bring the child to a realization of how far separate they are. At a time when it seems to him most important to be like his fellows, he is forced to realize his difference.

It is in the games which bring the two schools into contact that the differences between them are brought out most forcibly. In the capacity of audience the whole school body, graduates, and even parents of the students, are involved in the contest between the boys. In the state basketball tournament there are no more intensely fought games than those between the parochial and the public high schools. This intensity is increased by a feeling, on the part of many observers at least, that more than mere superiority in skill is here being demonstrated; no game is merely a game; it is, to some extent, an expression of opposition between two social groups in the community, two different religious groups. At one time feeling became so high during basketball games that the general public had to be barred from attendance; since that time the feeling has lessened greatly; but although it is better controlled, it still exists; the older members of the community still can read much into the game beyond this simple rivalry.

Their interpretation is strengthened to a certain extent by the difference in the way in which the two teams begin their play. The Burlington High School boys gather in a circle and plan their strategy. The Cathedral boys do the same; but as they finish, they say the "Our Father" and the "Hail Mary" and make the sign of the cross before entering the game. This, their coach says, is their own idea and does not come from any suggestion of his. It is primarily a prayer that they do their best and do nothing that is wrong or would reflect on their school, and that if it is the will of God, they should win; but to many of the audience, it looks as if they were praying for God to play on their side. This religious emphasis is obvious also on the baseball diamond. The Catholic boys not only pray before they begin the game, but as they go up to bat they make the sign of the cross in the sand before the home plate. At one game a disrespectful catcher of the public school's team would rub out the sign of the cross in front of the base before the pitcher threw his ball. A Jewish boy standing by, somewhat puzzled by the whole thing, remarked: "If they believe there is one God for all of us, how can they ask Him to grant them a special favor? And if they are praying to a special god of their own, how do they feel when he doesn't help them and they lose?"

The differences in the graduation exercises of the two schools also serve to show the different emphases. At the public high school Commencement, the principal speaker stressed the importance of meeting modern social problems with scientific objectivity. He pointed to Fascism, Communism, and our own "New Deal" and urged the students to recognize the desirability of experimentation. He ended with the advice to the students to "be themselves," adding that they were all endowed with free will and the ability to direct their course of action. At the parochial high school Commencement, a similar concern with social problems was evident, but the bishop, in speaking, stressed the fact that the disorganization in our modern life was due to the paganism which still existed in the world. He appealed to the graduating class for vocations to the priesthood and religious life, and he urged those that went on to college to choose Catholic colleges. "Moral education is utterly impossible outside of the Catholic schools today," he said. "Intellectual training is not the only important part, or even the important part of education." The other speaker at the exercise also emphasized the need for Christian living if the world is to solve its problems. His conclusion contrasts sharply with the individual emphasis of the public school speaker. According to the speaker at the parochial school exercises, "The Church of Christ has marked out for you the path; it will be for you so to live that you will leave a permanent impress upon the life about you, and make a real contribution to the peace and order of your own life and of society."

A small proportion of the students of each school go on to college, most of them to one of the two colleges in the town. The University of Vermont offers scholarships to pupils of high scholastic standing in both the high schools, but the decision before a boy from the Cathedral High School who wants to go on into the University rather than to the Catholic college is fraught with difficulty. He knows that he will meet different values in the University: history will be taught with a different emphasis; theories of evolution will be discussed; he may even come up against matters like sterilization and birth control. In addition, his adjustment to the social life of the University will be complicated; he will find that a great emphasis is still placed on fraternities, although this is lessening beneath the pressures of economic difficulties, and that few of the fraternities have room for a Catholic or a Jew. The consciousness of difference which may have been small in his high school life, where he did not often come up against the values of the Protestant world, will here be increased enormously. In addition, the fact that he is a Catholic will influence the girls he is going out with. If he goes with a Catholic girl, it will be assumed that his intentions are more serious than they would be if he were going with a Protestant girl, for he is reaching that age where the possibility of marriage must be considered, and the possibility of mixed marriage, as will be shown later, is still a remote one in Burlington. He may feel that the disadvantages of going to a college so firmly identified in his mind with Protestantism are too great, and in that case he will go to the near-by college of St. Michael's, where he will continue to be separated from the other group that makes part of the City of Burlington. His studies will continue to have a different emphasis, his social life will be more circumscribed, and he will be subject to none of the necessity for adjustment to a different world that he would have had to face, had he chosen differently.

In such a manner are the children of the community indoctrinated with different ideas, different ways of thought. Each school system is convinced that it has the one way of life which will produce the fine citizen; each is sure that it is fighting for values without which the world would be lost. The parochial school thinks it sees in the public school the threat of state-controlled education and looks upon itself as the great buffer against the regimentation latent in such a system. The public school, on the other hand, sees in the parochial school the continued domination of an ecclesiastical power and feels that it alone offers intellectual freedom. It is safe to say that neither one represents any safeguard against regimentation of thought; the choice is not between a free school and a controlled one, but between two kinds of control. As they exist today, side by side, whether one represents intellectual freedom and the other intellectual regimentation or not, they have, in Burlington at least, this result: they serve as a medium for perpetuating in the children of a diversified population a sense of difference.

CHAPTER VIII

THE COMMUNITY'S SOCIAL LIFE

THE democratic principles laid down by the founders of this country apparently die hard in a Puritan community. When a stranger first comes to Burlington, he may well be impressed by the friendly atmosphere which pervades the business section of the city. During the working day it would seem that Burlington is such a small world that nearly everyone knows everyone else. The cheery greetings on the street corners — "Hello, Charlie," "Good morning, Tom" — give the impression that people meet on a friendly basis unaffected by class distinctions. Moreover, the brief conversations overheard between the man who shines shoes and his customer, the clerk serving behind the counter and the restaurant manager, or the plumber, automobile salesman, newspaper man, and stockbroker who happen to share a table at lunchtime, convince one that these greetings arc more than merely "Hail fellow, well met," and are indeed the result of a certain knowledge and some appreciation of the life of each individual in the community.

With the end of the working day, however, something of this informality of acquaintanceship ceases. Some of the same people who greet each other informally in the morning give a more formal nod over their wives' shoulders if by chance they happen to meet in the evening at a movie, town concert, or lecture. This slight increase of formality affords a key to the bases of class distinctions which exist beneath the surface appearance of a fairly unified social world.

The actual division of Burlington's social life into a maze of classes and cliques is arbitrarily based on three kinds of differences apart from natural differences of interest. There is, first of all, the division based on differences in economic status which separate the community into two main groups — the working class and the business and professional class. A second large division is created by differences in religion which separate the community into the two main camps of Catholicism and Protestantism, each with its own social stratification along economic lines. The third division is based roughly on ethnic differences which serve to enhance the divisions based on religion or economic status and also to create division within the religious worlds or the economic levels.

Much of the ethnic division is understandable. The first and deepest relationships of each individual are connected with his family and those close to him. Throughout his childhood he is in a particular environment where certain modes of behavior and of thought are common; the standards of this first social world become deeply ingrained in him, and ever afterward he tends naturally to seek his friends among those whose traditions and standards are most like his own. These persons are likely to be of the same ethnic group as he is, as well as of the same economic level and religious group.

In considerations of American society, which is noted

for its mobility, the force of this unit in continuing into the second and third generation to determine the social world is sometimes neglected, yet something of the power of the ethnic group in providing a complete social life was revealed in the answers of the representatives of every group to the question "Of what nationality are your friends?" Among the 459 persons who were asked this question, the greatest proportion conscious of this group loyalty were of Old American, French-Canadian, and Jewish stock respectively. Of these the Old Americans are the most exclusive group. Eighty-seven per cent of those interviewed stated that they had intimate friends only among their own people. The only group nearing this degree of exclusiveness is the one usually considered most self-sufficient — the Jewish group. Seventy-four per cent of the Jews said that their social world was confined exclusively to their own group. The French Canadians, always considered the most clannish, were less so than either the Old Americans or the Jews. Only 60 per cent of their number claimed friends only among their own people.

In contrast to these three groups, the Italians, and especially the Germans and the Irish, felt that they included to a greater extent other people in their social world. Forty-three per cent of the Italians chose their friends exclusively within their own group, but only 21 per cent of the Germans and 23 per cent of the Irish did so.

Since so much of the deeply personal life of each individual in Burlington is confined within the ethnic group, it is important to know the activities of these groups. By analyzing them it should be possible to discover the extent to which activities are alike, and are unlike, behind ethnic fronts. To what extent do the social opportunities circumscribed within the ethnic worlds satisfy the social aspirations of the people? How rigid are the ethnic divisions within our society? What, in short, does the social life of each group mean, not only to the people of each group, but also to the community in general?

The social life of the Old Americans sets the social tone of the community. They are the charter members of society, and the rules that they make governing social intercourse are the rules that all others would follow. The activities of the Old Americans do not differ markedly from those of other groups, but their level of approach, it is felt, is on a higher plane; along with every other group, for example, the Old Americans go to the movies, but they go only to the "better" movies. They dance, but they do not attend public dances unless they sponsor them themselves. They play cards, but, as one French woman said, "Whereas the Old Americans play contract, the Irish play auction, and the French Canadians play whist." Through emulation this distinction is breaking down, but it indicates how the sense of social distance pervades the recreational activities of the people.

Within the group called Old American, forming as it does almost a caste, there are innumerable subdivisions and groupings based on curious social distinctions. Old American "Society" is composed of persons whose security of position derives from a complex of factors, including ethnic heritage, religious affiliation, a certain amount of wealth, a degree of educational advantage, subscription to certain standards of morality, and a record of long residence in the country or, even better, in the community. These are the people, living usually on the upper slope of the hill, augmented by socially acceptable persons connected with the University, that the community has in mind when it speaks of Old Americans, though they are really a small group behind the unity of Old America.

Although economically comfortable, members of this group like to believe that money is an unimportant factor in their position, but that instead their society is built on family traditions, qualities of character, civic leadership. Perhaps for this reason the group is conspicuously unostentatious in its manner and possessions. Only infrequently, when a ballet or play comes to town, are there chauffeured automobiles before the theatre or auditorium; then, Burlington is a little surprised to discover how many of its inhabitants can afford such luxuries; otherwise ostentation is not the manner of display of Burlington's leading social group. Their way of life is one of studied simplicity — old silver, old china, old furniture. No modern chromium or black glass invades Burlington's best homes. It is even rare for the women of this group to dress conspicuously well. The Jewish women, who are perhaps Burlington's best-dressed women, often comment with amazement on the lack of smartness and sophistication in the dress of many of the leading Old Americans. A

A HOME ON THE HILL

French-Canadian maid, however, arrived intuitively at an explanation with which the economist Thorstein Veblen would have agreed. She was telling her Old American employer that she needed a new coat for the spring. The Old American responded: "I don't see why you need another coat. Why, I am going to wear this same spring coat I've worn for six years." The French-Canadian maid replied: "You can afford to do so. You don't need to prove who you are by dressing well. The only way anyone can judge me is by the clothes on my back."

The social life of this group tends to be as simple as their appointments. Dinner parties are small, informal in tone, and easy. Conversation is on a light, impersonal level. The latest books are discussed; the issues that face the world are mentioned as one would mention something in which one is interested but not involved; or a new play, seen on a recent trip to Boston or New York, forms the basis for dinner conversation. Later, over the bridge table, discussion may involve the details of their daily life and their friends. "Gossip," said one Old American woman, "is one of our great sources of entertainment, only we like to think we are 'analyzing character' rather than talking about our neighbors." In this last activity the Old Americans are likely, as is every self-contained group, to make remarks on the assumption that everyone present is aware of the characteristics from schooldays on of the friend under discussion — an assumption usually justified, since there are not many strangers within the gates.

A considerable part of the activity of this group is devoted to patronizing the arts. Their names are first on the list at the circulating libraries for the more solid best sellers. They are faithful in attendance at community or university concerts and at lectures, the great proportion of which are on travel or other subjects remote from pressing social issues. They support a garden club which has occasional visiting speakers who talk on garden planning or flower arrangement. They sponsor art exhibits at the Fleming Museum, while there is a lively interest shown in local artists, and several members of the group try their hands at landscape and portrait painting, exhibits of their work alternating with others brought from the outside. Concerning their interest in art, one of their own group observed: "Their evaluation of any artistic effort is likely to be based on standards other than aesthetic; although, if a work does not offend their preconceptions, moral or political, they may then proceed to judge it aesthetically, sometimes with a good deal of justice." In this they are similar to all socially secure classes who, as R. M. MacIver points out, are inclined to promote all the more established artistic expressions "rather than the free intellectual activity which tends to question the *status quo.*" [1] Within the ranks of the Old Americans are many individuals who transcend the group pattern, question the *status quo,* think creatively about community or social problems, and even consider the possibility of a different and perhaps better Burlington. As long as they do not go too far with their

[1] *Society; Its Structure and Changes* (New York: R. Long and R. R. Smith, 1931), p. 94.

questioning, the group will uphold them; and they seldom do go too far, knowing the price they would have to pay.

To the community at large, this group gives two different impressions. The newcomer who is "accepted" by them is likely to express surprise at their difference from what he had expected. Instead of being cold or aloof, as Vermonters are reputed to be, they are hospitable, warm, and only slightly reserved. As long as the stranger meets the basic conventions and social codes required of good society, he finds a good deal of freedom and independence of expression. To such a newcomer Burlington seems one of the most delightful of residential cities. To the others within the community, however, who remain "outsiders," the Yankee group presents a different front. Some persons find it difficult to believe that its members are ever anything other than very well-mannered, but aloof and impersonal. They are baffled by their formalism and by the complex method of evaluation which determines whether or not people "belong."

Among the younger Old Americans, the "young married set" distinguish themselves from the "smart young married set." The two may intermingle, but the latter are more frequently to be found at cocktail parties, the Yacht Club dances, at bridge playing for money; whereas the "young married set" follow more clearly the pattern of behavior laid down by their ancestors. Their standard seems to be moderation. It is popular among this group at present to have children, at least two and possibly even three. They play bridge frequently, but seldom for money. They may enjoy a cocktail, but they do not go in for cocktail parties. A supper party or a lunch followed by bridge is the prevailing pattern; but for variety an occasional evening may be spent on a treasure hunt, or at a chicken pie supper in some rural church, or reviving old games, or having an informal dance. The older generation see in this division of the young people a separation that started during their own youth. As one woman remarked: "I can remember when we were first married there was our rather conservative crowd and another group that were interested more in the 'smart' things. Today, that crowd is still the older smart set in town, interested in golf and the Country Club, bridge and cocktail parties. Ours is more settled. The youngsters are going through the same pattern." There seems to be little inclination on the part of the children to break that pattern. The people they know are the sons and daughters of their parents' friends.

The clubs and societies to which the Old Americans belong set standards for the community. The social life of the group is more highly organized than that of any other except the Jewish. Eighty per cent of the men belong to clubs, some to as many as seven. Seventy-seven per cent of the women belong to clubs, some to as many as eight. A considerable number of these clubs are exclusively Old American and are expressive of class distinctions to an extent not found among other ethnic groups in the community. Intellectual interests are expressed in various informal discussion groups which range from the modestly titled "Chin-Chins" to the more self-assertive "Intelligentsia." The Chin-Chins read to each other through the winter such a book as Mrs. Gaskell's *Cranford,* after each session settling down to refreshments and informal discussion of any topic that may come up. The Intelligentsia, on the other hand, seriously tackle such books as *Moral Man in Immoral Society,* and discuss the social issues confronting the world today, the significance of social security measures, and so forth.

A few exclusive clubs which have long been a part of the social life of Old American "Society" continue to demonstrate the separatism of the Old Americans. Many of these clubs have been gradually beaten in upon by individuals from other ethnic groups or from other social classes in the community, but some still stand intact against such invasion.

Prominent among these are the many organizations of military origin. The presence of the Army Post within five miles is a strong influence in keeping these organizations alive and may be partially responsible for the fact that they are at present increasing in number. Membership in the longer established ones, such as the Daughters of the American Revolution, the Society of Colonial Wars in the State of Vermont, and the Daughters of the Union Veterans of the Civil War, demands long residence in the country. The Daughters of the American Revolution is perhaps the most active of these particular patriotic societies. Its interest in patriotism and national defense is kept alive by the enthusiasm of the women whose husbands have been identified with the military post or have held high position in the Army. The Citizenship Committee is ever anxious to find new directions for its activities. It visits the courts when immigrants become citizens and presents each new citizen with a flag and with a book on citizenship. Its members visit the schools, particularly on patriotic occasions, and they show especial interest in the parochial schools. To them all they give flags and prizes — to the child who writes the most acceptable essay on citizenship, or, in the elementary school, to the child who, in the judgment of his teachers and fellow pupils, has deported himself in a manner becoming an ideal citizen. In addition to this, they are concerned with remembering the important patriotic holidays in the year, preserving historical spots, and seeing to it that old graveyards are kept in order.

About 1934, the monthly programs of this organization showed a great deal of concern with the dangers its members felt were facing America. Some of the topics discussed were "Old Glory versus Red," "Sinister Shadows," and "The Constitution of the United States." More recently they have been less aggressive in defending their particular version of Americanism in their meetings, and the topics discussed have been less militantly patriotic; "Forestry Conservation versus Forestry," "Genealogical Records," "The Moving Picture of Today and Tomorrow," "Three American Shrines." With all their activity, however, the Daughters of the American Revolution do not hold the important social place in Burlington that they do in smaller communities. They are a group of some seventy women, many of whom are too old to attend meetings. It is only on particular occasions that the rest of the community becomes aware of the organization's potential influence in determining the type of patriotism in the community. Such an occasion arose in Burlington recently when the moral support of the Daughters of the American Revolution strengthened the insistence of the American Legion on the passage of the Teachers' Oath bill in the State Legislature.

Of the more purely social clubs, one which has altered little in the character of its membership since its organization in 1869, is The Neighbors, a selected group of Old American families who meet once a month to read plays. Each month a family acts as host to the other families and is responsible for the selection of a play. Formerly the meetings were held in the various homes; but now, much to the regret of many members, the meetings are held in the rooms of one of the more exclusive clubs of the city. The meetings have an undoubted charm, arising partly from the feeling of assurance and well-being which is characteristic of any gathering of people who "belong" and are not likely to do or think anything that "is not done." The members usually dress in evening clothes, and occasionally those who are to participate in the reading assume the costumes which they feel fits the characters they are to read. There is frequently a good deal of trouble in selecting the plays, since many of the older members are prone to resent any intimation of immorality, but some very pleasing choices which cannot disturb the most conservative taste are frequently made — the Jerome dramatization of *Pride and Prejudice,* a cut version of *The Taming of the Shrew,* a dramatization of Stevenson's *Lodging for a Night.* One evening was spent in reading excerpts from some of the early American plays, such as *Pocahontas* and *Our American Cousin.* When the reading is over, the members move about and discuss over their ice cream and cake the good and bad points of the play and the interpretations of the various persons who took part. The group usually begins to disband about 10:30; eleven o'clock is still a late hour in older Burlington's best social set.

In a club with such a strong social emphasis, the basis on which members are selected is complicated. Inheritance plays a part in filling the membership, but beyond that few are able to define precisely the qualifications which an individual aspiring to membership should possess. Certainly an ability to read plays is of secondary importance to the more intangible characteristics which go to make up a socially "acceptable" person.

Another society, as exclusive, is the Friends-in-Council, organized in 1878. This is thought to be the oldest women's club in the state, but it does not wish to join with the State Federation of Women's Clubs and remains limited in membership, taking in new members only when vacancies occur through death or removal. A distinction in which it takes particular pride is that it still follows the form of procedure established fifty-eight years ago; at the home at which a meeting is being held there hangs on the door a sign which reads, "Friends-in-Council," and the Friends do not knock but enter unannounced. The main activity of this group is study, and a good deal of research has usually gone into the papers that are presented. When a subject has been selected, it usually serves for a number of years. During the past two years, for example, Scandinavia has been considered with a thoroughness that contrasts sharply with such studies in other groups. Excellent papers have been prepared on the coöperative movement in Sweden and Denmark and on the system of government in these countries, and talks on leaders of thought at various periods in Scandinavian history have been presented. Certain of these subjects are, however, presented with some hesitancy, such as the life of Ellen Keyes and her theories of marriage, love, and raising children. Such theories as she held are not yet a matter of common drawing-room conversation in Burlington, and to have to give unconventional interpretations, even though in the name of study, is embarrassing to both the speaker and the audience.

The basis on which gaps in membership are filled is not fixed. Intellectual curiosity may be a part of it, but that other considerations enter is indicated by the remark of one member who explained that a few "socially wrong" people have somehow managed to slip into the group. Thus far it has remained free of any members that are "ethnically wrong."

A social organization of outstanding significance in measuring class and ethnic distance is the Klifa Club, the leading women's social club of the city. It grew out of a small literary club which met upstairs in one of the business buildings and from this circumstance was given the Icelandic name *Klifra,* or Climbers', Club, which by mistake became Klifa. In the early history of the club its waiting list was long and membership was on a highly selective basis. It was seldom that anyone concerning whose social standing there was any question could gain admission; with only one exception, no member of an ethnic group other than Old American measured up to the social standards set. In more recent years, however, because of the increasing number of social organizations which meet the needs of women of this class, the club has found itself with a diminished waiting list and has accordingly extended its qualifications for membership to include persons from the general American Protestant and even Roman Catholic groups concerning whose social standing or congeniality there previously might have been some question. As the club has become inclusive rather than exclusive, cliques have formed, at least one of which is along religious lines. Among some of the older members there is a bewildered feeling that the whole thing has gotten rather out of hand and that the name of the club now has a connotation other than that originally intended. Feeling this, they have tended to withdraw more and more from active interest in the club as those with greater social needs have advanced.

The Klifa Club, however, still keeps its place in the life of the community; the social columns of the newspapers give prominent space to its activities. It distinguishes itself from the Athena Club, its closest rival in social leadership, by priding itself on being wholly social and unconcerned with the studying which is one of the Athena Club's chief interests. As some of the Klifa Club members explained: "The Athena Club is for those women who still feel they need to study and improve their minds. The Klifa Club members don't have to do that to gain social place in the community." The Klifa Club also distinguishes itself from most other social clubs in the community by refusing to take out membership in the Vermont Federation of Women's Clubs. Its programs place primary emphasis upon entertainment. It brings in speakers, singers, and musicians to entertain its members. Such authors as Stephen Leacock, Zona Gale, Frances Frost, and Ludwig Lewisohn have addressed the members in recent years. Talks on gardens of Italy and how etchings are made have been interspersed with instrumental or vocal music.

Many other organizations serve the Old American group in fact; but although organized by this group, they are meant to serve all persons in the community qualified for membership. These will be considered later. The exclusive clubs, of which The Neighbors is illustrative, represent the most determined desire on the part of the Old Americans to be self-contained. The charm and sense of security of such a closed social world on the one hand is offset by its influence on the rest of the community. Even while its pattern of life is admired and emulated by other groups, its closed doors tend to set up standards of superiority and inferiority unrelated to standards of worth and character. In addition, they act as a strong force for social stability that is sometimes indistinguishable from immobility.

The Jewish world is as distinct as is the Old American. The Jews are so traditionally a self-contained group that the impression prevails in Burlington that "they like to be by themselves," and whether or not this is true, the belief is a comforting one to those who are not anxious to see the Jews included to any extent in the general social life of the community.

There are, however, some curious contradictions in the social life of the Jews. In appearance and manner they are like every other group in the community; their women are the most smartly dressed, they play bridge, dance, and golf; as a group they are second only to the Old Americans in the support they give to the cultural activities of the city. The manager of one of the circulating libraries in town said: "The taste of the Jews is better than that of any other group, including the Old Americans. They are more curious intellectually, and they are not so afraid of finding a new idea in a book." Yet, within their own world their social life centers around religious rituals characteristic of Jewish tradition. There are adaptations made, it is true, to the demands of our complex civilization, but the old forms, though modified, persist. Thus, in keeping with modern medical trends, babies are born in hospitals rather than at home, and circumcision, performed a week later, does not assume quite the same festive character as it did when it took place at home; but parties are held in the hospitals, the godfather and godmother proudly display the new baby, and the mother is visited in her hospital room by relatives and friends.

At about six years of age, immediately after the public school day is over, boys and girls attend the Hebrew Free School, where they learn the language and customs and the religious beliefs of their people. In the few families who no longer keep kosher house, this first sending of their children to the Hebrew School is a time of conflict. The young boy returns to argue with his mother that pork is unclean, that she shouldn't have bacon for breakfast, that she should have two sets of dishes, one for foods containing milk and one for foods containing meat. Leaders of the group may lament the fact that all the children of the community do not come for as many years as they should to Hebrew Free School, but with only a few exceptions, all parents send their children there at least for a short period prior to their reaching the age of thirteen. This represents the age at which the boys are admitted to manhood and is again a festive occasion. There is a great deal of preparation of foods for days in advance. Practically the entire Jewish community is invited; gifts are presented to the boy; he chants a section of the Bible, makes a brief speech, and thus becomes an adult member of the Jewish congregation.

Weddings are observed with only a few minor changes

in the traditional manner. With few exceptions they are held either in the synagogue or in a hall. The wedding ceremony takes place beneath a canopy, and even though the bride's veil be but a brief, transparent one, the ceremony of unveiling her and revealing her to the groom is included. The rabbi beseeches the newly married couple to remember that though they may not be able to live up to all the Jewish customs in this western world, they should remember that they are Jews and abide by certain of the most important customs at least. Feasting and usually dancing follow. Throughout life, in most cases, the couple abide by the dietary laws of the group, and the husband performs the obligations in the synagogue becoming to the head of the household. There are a few families who no longer adhere to these customs, but these few — even though some of them may be the leading members of the group — are looked at askance, especially by the older members, who frequently refuse to break bread in their homes because they are "unclean"; and the very smallness of the group enables such group pressure to be keenly felt. At a death the members of the Holy Society keep watch and pray until the time of burial. A movement to alter the burial procedure to embalming and use of a casket was opposed; funeral processions are conducted according to the old tradition.

In addition to these ritual aspects of their lives, the Jews have many social organizations to keep alive the spirit and the law of Judaism. For the 215 families there are more than thirteen clubs serving their group exclusively.

Most of the group belong to three clubs, but some to as many as nine.

For the children there are three Zionist organizations, divisions of the Young Judaea for different age groups. For the young people there are particularly the Yiddish Student Culture Club and the Masada, where subjects related in any way to Jewish life and culture of the present and the past are brought for discussion. For the women there are the Ladies' Aid Society, concerned primarily with raising money for the needy, and a local branch of the National Council for Jewish Women, a study and social club. In this club, topics of varied interest pertaining to Jewish life are studied and programs appropriate to the important Jewish holidays are held. Studies of the early Bible history of the Jewish people and of anti-Semitism are interspersed with general topics on social welfare, public health, and the part that Jewish women can play in larger civic concerns of city and the State.

For the men there are the B'nai B'rith and the Knights of Pythias. While the latter provides a social atmosphere in which the members of the club can feel comfortably at home, the B'nai B'rith is the *sine qua non* of membership in the Jewish elite circles. In addition to its purely social function as a club, the B'nai B'rith has presented many lecturers to its members. There have been talks on Palestine, Iceland, and Russia among others, and talks and a debate upon Zionism. All of these organizations have as one of their major concerns the raising of money for the care and protection of those in need. Besides, either individual members of the clubs or the clubs as a whole send money to Palestine or elsewhere where Jews are in need. They also support Jewish institutions throughout this country, and through the Vermont Branch of the Zionist Organization of America are connected with a movement international in aim. In addition there are a few organizations directly connected with the synagogue.

There have been several branches of other national organizations functioning at one time or another in the community, such as the Young Men's Hebrew Association, the Young Women's Hebrew Association, and the Junior Council of Jewish Women, but the group, though willing, is not large enough to maintain any more organizations. The complexity of those already existing in such a small community and their strict adherence to lines of race and religion mirror the determination of the Jews to preserve the integrity of their group. In addition, the nature of these clubs means that for the average Jew there is, as for the average member of no other group, a wider horizon of interest extending beyond the boundaries of the community and identifying him with all Jews everywhere in a cultural unity.

In spite of the high degree of organization within the Jewish group, the forces for disintegration that affect every ethnic group in America are at work. One significant indication is the decline in the use of Yiddish in the home. Only four of the fifty-seven Jewish householders interviewed — and these four all of the first generation — speak nothing but Yiddish at home. In thirteen homes the parents speak Yiddish almost entirely, but the children speak both Yiddish and English; in ten homes Yiddish and English are used interchangeably; while in thirty English is the language generally spoken, although Yiddish is occasionally used. Among the second generation of this group, the English language has almost entirely supplanted the Yiddish, which is used only to express favorite idiomatic phrases.

The change in language is only one indication of other changes that are taking place. In spite of the many organizations and the ritual of their daily life, the pressure occasioned by living in a community where Jewish customs frequently conflict with more general ones makes it impossible for many people to keep their customs as they might wish. Among the younger generation, for example, dietary customs observed in the home may be neglected outside it. Many Jewish traditions are maintained in symbolic rather than in literal form. On the other hand, pressures from both within and without the group keep the Jew in the main to his traditional role. As one leading Jewish woman explained, "The Gentile community expect that I keep kosher house. They take it for granted that I would not eat pork, and I feel that it is my duty therefore to prove to them that I am a good Jew even if these customs do not necessarily mean anything much to me any more." At the same time, the group is so small that it, too, exerts considerable pressure on its wayward members. This is possible in a community where, if the members of one group deviate from its customs or break its taboos, they cannot easily find another group to accept them or make them feel at home.

Thus the struggle for freedom of thought and independence within the Jewish group is similar to, but more intense than, that within the Old American. It is a conflict within a family, based on differences in the importance attached to forms. A real change in one's way of life to a completely different form of conduct is achieved at too great a price for most people. Recently, in addition, recognizing that being Jewish is still a "problem" in the world, many Jews have come closer to their traditional ways in order that the integrity of the group may be a safeguard against the possible time when they may be reminded by the community that they are a group apart. Hence, forms are frequently preserved after the content has ceased to have meaning.

For these reasons, social relations which imply real friendship between Jew and Gentile are not common and are discouraged by both Gentile and Jew. The Gentile imagines that the Jews are so unified that "if you know one Jew you have to know them all, and so you soon find you don't know any of your own kind." The Jews fear that their unity, which has been found valuable so often in the past, will be broken down. Hence any friendship, especially between the younger members of the two groups, is usually surreptitious and unsatisfactory. Occasionally a Jewish boy and a Christian girl, whose interest in each other has caused them to disregard the community taboo, may be seen slipping into a moving picture theatre where, they hope, the darkness may conceal them. Thus the whole problem of the Jew in making a deeply satisfying social adjustment to two worlds — that of his own group, and that of the general American community — is for some individuals unbelievably complicated. Part of this complication is undoubtedly the result of the size of the town — large enough to have a Jewish "group" and a Jewish section, small enough to be aware of any attempt to move out of either. As one Jewish woman who had come to town from elsewhere commented: "I had never before been compelled as I have been here to limit my circle of friends only to Jews. I have never felt such pressure on me as a Jew, both from within my group and from the community at large. In a big city one makes a freer choice of friends. Here you are put in just one group, the Jews, and the community sees that you stay there." Beneath this pressure the majority conform, and confine their intimate social life to their own group. A few stand alone, lost between two worlds, one of which they have rejected, in the other of which they are not accepted; even fewer make a more or less satisfactory adjustment to both worlds.

In marked contrast to the urban, highly organized Jewish social life is the social life of the French Canadians. No other group is less organized; only some 46 per cent of the men and 39 per cent of the women belong to any clubs. Organization has never, in the past, been a feature of their lives. Many look back wistfully to a day when their social life was intimate and gay and satisfactorily self-contained. In every family there was some one who could play a fiddle, someone who could dance a jig; all could sing. When neighbors gathered, which they did more frequently than they do now, it was not long before someone would strike up the fiddle; and young and old would dance and sing. On Sunday after church many of them spent the rest of the day in a park near Archibald Street, bringing their lunches and all their children. But, along with every other group, the French Canadians have been affected by the change in the type of amusements and the substitution of the automobile and the moving picture for neighborhood visits. As one woman lamented: "We don't know our neighbors any more. They own a car, we own a car. Whenever my husband has spare time, we take a little trip in our car. We don't go calling." The music of professional radio artists now replaces the less skillful, if more enthusiastic, efforts of their own people. This mechanization of music affects even those who have no radios. On a Saturday night on North Street, many French-Canadian men, women, and children are to be seen standing silently outside a beer garden through whose open windows come the strains of the latest hill-billy songs.

In spite of these social changes, however, there are forces which contribute to preserving a distinct French-Canadian social life. For example, with their radios they are able to tune in on French stations in Canada, and so to maintain their identification with their own race to an extent not permitted other groups of foreign heritage. The automobile means that they are only three or four hours from Montreal and the French settlements of Canada. In addition, they are able to keep alive their interest in the culture of their own people through subscription to the various papers which speak for the whole French-Canadian group, such as *L'Union, Le Travailleur,* and *La Presse,* even though their local paper, *Le Patriote Canadien,* the first French-Canadian newspaper in the United States, has long since been discontinued.

Yet there are many indications that the daily social life of the French-Canadian Americans is becoming progressively less different from that of their fellow Americans. Old-timers recall the days when the twenty-fourth of June, the day of Saint Jean Baptiste, the patron saint of the French Canadians, was a gala day with parades through the streets of the city and speeches rife with such phrases as "the great and glorious French-Canadian race." This celebration, however, has entirely died down except within the French-Canadian community of Lakeside, where an attempt at a parade around the square is still made on that day. French Canadians themselves account for this decline by a decline in nationality interest among those of French-Canadian descent and in part by the half-amused criticism and lack of appreciation shown by the citizens as a whole toward this celebration.

A further sign of change is to be noted in the fact that New Year's is for most French Canadians no longer the occasion for a celebration as extensive as it used to be in Quebec. Today, in few Burlington French-Canadian households is the father's blessing asked at New Year's.

There has been a shift from the French emphasis on *Heureuse Année* to emphasis on the more American *Joyeux Noël*.

One of the chief disintegrating influences is the loss of the distinctive language. With the increased use of radios this may not progress so rapidly as it did before it was possible to listen to French throughout the day. Today, however, only 9 per cent of the representative group interviewed in detail speak only French in the home. In an additional 12 per cent of the homes the parents speak French almost entirely but the children speak both English and French or only English; in 34 per cent of the homes both languages are used to an equal extent; while in the remaining 45 per cent, English is the predominant, and usually the only, language. This increasing use of English not only indicates an already extensive contact with other groups, but seems to point to a future in which the sense of social separation of ethnic groups will not be enhanced by a difference in language.

Coincident with this gradual loss of language, many of the second- and third-generation Americans of the French-Canadian group, particularly among those who have achieved some degree of economic security, lose most of the peasant qualities characteristic of the group as a whole, and qualities considered to be more French predominate. Gentleness and simplicity remain, but to these are added an element of quiet sophistication and gentility. This is partially the result of an increased interest in France and an appreciation on a higher level of the traditions and manners of that remote homeland. A certain reserved pride seems to take the place of the feeling of inferiority characteristic of those whose position in the community is less assured.

Even in that part of French-Canadian social life which is organized, there are indications that the pressure of living in a complex community is tending to offset the pressure exerted by those members of the ethnic group who would like to see the French Canadians more self-contained. The Saint-Jean-Baptiste Society, organized as early as 1872 with the purpose of mutual aid to its members and aid to any French Canadian in regard to any problem connected with immigration, gradually yielded to a national organization — L'Union Saint-Jean-Baptiste — whose insurance aspects on a national scale would embrace all French Canadians, and which has therefore won over many of the small independent units. Even L'Union, however, is not so strong as it once was. Many of the men have explained that if it wasn't for its insurance aspects it couldn't be kept alive. True, in the south end of town, in the cotton-mill section, it still is the only French social organization outside of the church; and it has, therefore, a proportionately high membership — 240 persons. In the older section of town the 500 members constitute a small proportion of the French Canadians located there. The women's auxiliary is considerably more active than the men's, having an average attendance at meetings of sixty, whereas that at the men's is forty-five. But in neither of the meetings do French and French-Canadian interests predominate; the program, rather, is determinedly like that of every other group in the community. After the business is completed, the meetings resolve themselves into card parties or bingo games to raise money, or into social hours during which people sit around and talk and have refreshments.

The only French-Canadian organization which does not have any religious affiliation is the Ligue des Patriotes Franco-Americaines, founded by a group of women in 1918 to do war work. Subsequently the organization thus begun made a not-very-successful effort to encourage French-Canadian music and plays; today it maintains clubrooms where elderly women meet to play whist and to engage in other forms of entertainment, and it also does a certain amount of charitable work.

The fact that a relatively small proportion of the French-Canadian social life is organized has a twofold effect on the French Canadian's position in respect to the social life of the community. It means that there are few mediums through which the French Canadian can be reached when any social project of the community as a whole is contemplated, but on the other hand, the difficulty experienced in maintaining a nationalistic society or in forming new nationalistic societies for those of French-Canadian stock perhaps indicates a closer approach to the more general American life than either the French Canadians would care to admit or the other ethnic groups have been able to see. Within their own group, the French Canadians are having to make innumerable adjustments between their tendency toward ethnic integrity and the environmental forces compelling them to identify themselves with the life of America.

The Italians, although they are more self-contained than either the Germans or the Irish, are more consciously determined to become an acceptable element in the community than perhaps any other small group. Not until recently has their social life been organized on any ethnic basis, perhaps because the few families from the northern part of Italy were slow to become willing to work with the more numerous families from the southern part. In 1933, however, the Twin City Italian Club was organized, and since its organization has flourished. At present renting a clubhouse in the Italian neighborhood, it has already bought a lot on which it plans to build. Very significantly, the monthly programs of this club, instead of being devoted to the glory of Italy, put emphasis on the fact that the Italians here are all American citizens. They attack with great earnestness the problem of learning the customs and laws of the country in which they now live; their speakers are usually men connected with city, state, or national government who are asked to explain the various functions of government without any political flavor. The older men who have not learned English are sometimes suspicious of these English speakers until other members explain to them the nature of the talk. The club also has various books and pamphlets to explain questions of citizenship. Its major interests, however, are social. It has a beer license; and an Italian orchestra provides the music for dancing and singing.

When some members find it difficult to meet the high membership fee of a dollar a month, a small group of men within the club help to tide them over until they are able to pay. The Italian group as a whole looks upon the club as a great new lease of life for itself and an important expression of participation in the community.

The club, however, serves primarily the needs of the men of the group. The women are expected to attend only at social functions. There is still a strong conservative feeling that the women should remain at home and find their recreation in embroidering and crocheting as their mothers did in Italy. They may visit with each other in the evenings, but their main social expression is expected to be within the family; and since the families are fairly large, few of the women have time for much activity outside.

The impact of American life has nevertheless penetrated into the Italian home through the men, who feel it in their working world, and the children, who feel it in the schools. In regard to language alone, in only eight of the homes of the thirty-six families interviewed is Italian alone spoken. All of these homes are of first-generation householders. In eleven of the homes, although the parents speak Italian, the children either speak Italian to their parents and English among themselves, or only English at all times. In seven of the homes, both parents and children speak English and Italian interchangeably. In ten, English is the language used, although Italian may be spoken occasionally.

This loss of language is partially the result of the small-ness of the group. Throughout the day the contacts of its members are largely with members of other groups. To their small number may also be laid the fact that the Italians do not have the same social expression that larger groups in the city find. Their feast days may be celebrated within the homes, but the group is far too small to indulge in the gala celebrations that make the lives of their com-patriots in other cities more colorful. These things con-tribute to their desire to be identified with the larger American community, and to find therein a social expres-sion which their limited number prevents them from find-ing alone. By a majority of the other ethnic groups, however, the Italian is still held suspect, and as long as this attitude of prejudice persists it is doubtful if he will be permitted to make a contribution to the social life of the community as colorful as he is capable of.

The social activities of the Germans have been organized around the Goethe Lodge of the German Order of Haru-gari, a branch of a mutual aid organization for all Germans in America. For the older Germans this club was the very center of their life, but in the second generation it has been increasingly difficult to preserve German culture as zeal-ously as the first generation strove to do. The Germans are among the groups most rapidly assimilated; although by choice many of them prefer to live their social life within their own group. They identify themselves, how-ever, in thought at least, with the larger community so quickly that by the second generation English is spoken almost exclusively, and even in the first generation no one speaks German exclusively. In addition, they are considered by the other ethnic groups among the most socially acceptable of all. These factors combine to produce a broad interest that extends beyond the group, so that those who regret the slackening of interest in the club can do very little about it.

Meetings are held bimonthly for both the men's organization and the women's auxiliary, although on different days. One talk during the entire year may be, for example, as last year, on "My Experiences in Germany during the World War," a talk by a college professor, but the other subjects are of general interest to any Americans. Such subjects as the following were, for example, part of last year's program: "Tammany Hall in New York," "My Adventures in the Philippines," "Pages out of my Army Life." Thus the club's original function has faded into the background. In order to assure its very existence, social membership has been established. A bar and frequent dances attract a considerable number of French Canadians, of Irish, and of other groups in the neighborhood. This new arrangement has made possible the continuation of the club and given it a new lease of life, but it is a different life from that which its founders originally planned.

Of all the social worlds in the community, that of the Irish is the most completely denationalized. For them the original barrier of language did not exist; and so, although they are separated from Old American society, the barriers are socio-religious rather than ethnic. Behind these barriers the social pattern of their life is very similar to that of the Old Americans. Certainly there is a leading social set among the Irish as there is among the Old Americans. At times they join with members of the Old American group, but this is almost always at large impersonal bridge parties, teas, or other similar functions. The more personal social life of each is behind the walls of its own group. The conservative Old American may recognize the fact that many of the Irish are on the same economic level as himself, but the Irish "top" society is not quite comparable with the same level of Old American society. Occasionally Old Americans are heard to point out certain individuals within the Irish group who now would be acceptable in Old American society, commenting at the same time that that is a possibility that has only occurred within the last ten or fifteen years. But the Irish, meanwhile, recognizing that the doors are slightly ajar, are somewhat less interested than they were in getting through. They prefer to build their own social life, at least until the doors are opened wide.

The remark of one Irish woman, who has been considered acceptable in Old American society, illustrates this. "Like everybody else in town, I used to think it would be nice to be a member of Burlington's high society, but after I had been made welcome in the finest homes on the hill I discovered that I preferred my relatives and the friends I had known since childhood, and, as I got older, to watch their children come along. Being a member of Society has ceased to have any meaning to me."

The other side of the picture is that as the Old Americans hold aloof from any deeply personal social life with the Irish, the Irish in turn seem equally aloof from the French Canadians. The door of the Irish elite social life is not open to many of the elite from the French-Canadian world.

No truly nationalistic organization now represents the unity of the Irish group in Burlington. The Hibernian Society, organized in 1900 as a mutual aid society for Irish immigrants, was not able to last through the World War. An Irishman explained this by saying that "there was no time then to root just for the Irish." Perhaps as a substitute for such nationalistic organizations the Irish have acquired recognized leadership in such religious organizations as the Knights of Columbus, which they established in the community for all Catholics. In general, as a group, they are the leaders of Catholic social life as the Old Americans are of the community social life.

Thus does the ethnic group define the social world for many people. It answers specific needs and supplies the individual with a group, the values of which are known and established, and within which he finds the same sense of support that he finds in his family. But beyond this, the distinctions between group and group are, to a large extent, purely formal. The social organizations of the French Canadians, the Germans, the Italians, and the Irish are quite similar. They answer few distinctly ethnic needs. Rather is there a striving toward standardization, an attempt to achieve a pattern of behavior that shall be indistinguishable from what they consider to be good American society. Yet in spite of this, the separation persists, even expressing itself in such simple social gestures as going to the moving pictures: members of every group find amusement at the movies, but they find it at different movie houses, two of which serve primarily the French-Canadian and other less established economic groups, and two primarily the Old Americans, the Irish, and the University students.

This persistence of a formal pattern of separation after its reason for existence has largely disappeared has two effects on the community. On the one hand, it gives to the community an appearance of stability which derives from the individual's sense of security in his daily social life. On the other hand, it makes for social inertia because of the tendency to place a premium upon conformity to the mores of a small group. When an individual attempts to reach outside his own group, the weight not only of his own group but also of the community at large is to some extent set against him. Under such pressure, many personalities which would expand in a friendlier atmosphere have become warped and little, jealous and thwarted. The energy that might go into leadership, if their society placed value on qualities other than conformity, becomes dissipated and drawn off into fruitless discussion and criticism. That this compulsion exists in the community even today is to be seen in the extent to which people agreed, disagreed, or were uncertain about the following statement: "One is criticized by one's own nationality group if one mixes freely with people of other nationalities in the community." The fact that one half of the whole group interviewed agreed with the statement and an additional one tenth were uncertain is an interesting reflection of the strength of this social taboo.

The variation of the power of this force among the several groups is of still further interest. The French Canadians are apparently most conscious of this form of group pressure, for almost two thirds of their number agreed with the statement. The Old Americans were a close second; over one half — 55 per cent — registered their assent. The Irish, the Germans, and the Jews are all about equally conscious of the pressure of their groups, two fifths of each group agreeing with the statement. On the other hand, among the Italians, who are almost entirely of the first generation, only one fourth agreed.

The feeling that there is a social taboo against making friends among other ethnic groups increases rather than decreases with each generation. Forty-one per cent of the first generation feel it, 49 per cent of the second, and 55 per cent of the third. This varies from group to group, but only the Irish show a marked decrease in consciousness of this taboo from one generation to the next. The general increase, however, may not mean that the social pressure is any greater, but merely a greater consciousness of the taboo as the individual first comes in contact with a social world larger than that of his group.

In opposition to this taboo, innumerable forces tend to offset the pressure making for the social separation of groups. One of these forces is the very nature of the development of the social life within each group. Behind barriers, the social life of each tends to develop along very similar lines. As these similarities become more and more apparent, the barriers of ethnic separation tend to break down. New groups based on a larger interest or a different interest are formed either as substitutes for the ethnic world or to hold the equal or even greater interest of the individual.

The first new basis for an enlarged social world is likely to be one which embraces ethnic and even class differences within a single powerful unit of culture. Usually this unit is religious. French Canadians, Irish, and Italians discover that in spite of their differences they are bound together by a strong force — their common religion. The formal expression of this is best seen in such organizations as the Knights of Columbus and the Catholic Daughters of America — societies which combine representatives of all the Catholic ethnic groups in the name of their religion.

The Knights of Columbus, for example, carries on an extensive program along religious, educational, and patriotic lines for all Catholic members. Its bimonthly meetings are frequently devoted to hearing a speaker on some topic of general interest, especially on current events, European conditions, and so forth. A professor from the University of Vermont or St. Michael's College is frequently the main speaker. Since the opening of the Y. M. C. A. Community Center, there have been developed additional activities for the younger men. The Cathedral High School gymnasium is opened to the members weekly, and bowling tournaments and debates are leading attractions.

Yet this organization has trouble in keeping up the interest of members. Though 350 men are enrolled, the average attendance at meetings is forty-five; cliques are formed, and these tend to be along ethnic lines. To the French Canadian, the Knights of Columbus is an Irish organization, and efforts made by the Irish to counteract this impression have seldom been much more successful than have been the efforts of Old Americans to make members of a minority group feel at home in organizations under Old American leadership. In such situations a few persons of the minority group mingle easily with both groups, but many shrink back because of a real or imagined feeling of being discriminated against. Thus many French Canadians, although represented in the Knights of Columbus, feel more at home in such organizations as the Woodmen and the Eagles.

In a similar way the Catholic Daughters of America meet the social needs of many Irish, French-Canadian, and even some Italian women. Their primary interest is in social service, but they also sponsor Convert League meetings and have a study club. This club, though more liberal than such an Old American group as the Athena Club in that they have had discussions of communism, socialism, capitalism, and so forth, have studied not the economic and social ideals of these movements so much as their relation to Roman Catholicism.

In spite of these common interests of the members of the club, ethnic differences have asserted themselves here as in the Knights of Columbus. As one French-Canadian woman said: "At card parties, when the Irish women play bridge in one room, we play whist in another. And even though we may be learning to play auction, the Irish are learning to play contract — so in general we still don't get together."

In addition to these major social clubs are the numerous other societies more directly connected with the church and the parochial schools. For the young girls there is the Children of Mary Society, for their older sisters the Sodality of the Virgin Mary, and for their mothers the St. Anne's Society and the Mothers Club connected with the parochial high school. The men have such organizations as the St. Vincent de Paul Society; the boys, altar societies and, for those in the University, the Newman Club. The Newman Club has Communion breakfasts, occasional boat rides, and speakers.

In spite of the fact that consciousness of ethnic difference does arise, particularly within the larger religious societies, the very fact that these organizations do continue to draw membership from all Catholic groups, and that some individuals make a satisfactory adjustment within a world thus larger than that of the ethnic group, points to a developing sense of common interests.

The Protestants of the community also have their organizations set up on a religious base. In a sense, their churches themselves are social as well as religious units, but in addition there are within each church numerous clubs, such as choirs, women's guilds, men's brotherhoods, missionary societies, and Bible study groups, whose activities provide for some church members a complete social world. There is also at least one organization, the King's Daughters, which makes a deliberate attempt through several "Circles" to bind the members of a number of Protestant churches into a unit, but the tendency is for a great representation of one church to be in each Circle of the society. This makes for a certain division within the society different from that within a comparable Catholic society in that social distinctions are not enhanced by ethnic differences. The opening ode for all meetings of the various Circles within the King's Daughters indicates their main aims: "God helping us, we will watch our thoughts, words, and actions. God helping us, we will do some act of kindness each day to or for some individual." Following a business meeting and the singing of hymns, and perhaps a solo or duet, the Circle may listen to someone talk on the importance of the Children's Aid Society to the State, or the work of the policewoman, or some such subject. Meanwhile, the members all sit around and tear sheets, fold hems, and roll bandages for the Mary Fletcher Hospital. Members of various Protestant congregations also meet when the missionary societies unite in an annual meeting or at such a time as Holy Week, when the leading churches unite in daily service.

The organizations most strongly identified with Protestant Americanism, however, are the Y. M. C. A. and the

Y. W. C. A. Irrespective of how secular they have become, with their character-building program concentrated primarily in recreational activities, it will be a long time before, in Burlington, they are dissociated from Protestantism. Other organizations which are identified with the Protestant group are the Masonic order and its auxiliary, the Eastern Star, and to a lesser degree the Odd Fellows and their related society, the Rebekahs. This identification is not entirely justified, although the reasons for it are indicated in Chapter vi. Jews, for example, belong both to the Y. M. C. A. Community Center and to the Masonic Lodge, although some speak of difficulty in gaining admission to the latter. An indication of the way in which organizations supposedly non-sectarian tend to become identified with one religious group is afforded by such an organization as the Knights of Pythias, which in Burlington has two separate lodges, one Jewish and the other Protestant.

Though it may seem that religious affiliation should not play an important part in determining the limits of social life, yet it was found that for a considerable number of Burlingtonians social horizons are bounded by the barriers which separate the three main religious groups, Catholic, Protestant, and Jewish. Throughout, this was more true of the women than of the men. This limitation appears in the following percentages, which represent the membership of the persons in each group in clubs either directly connected with a church or limited in membership to one religious or ethnic group.

In the Jewish group, 59 per cent of the men's membership in clubs, and 78 per cent of the women's, is confined
to Jewish organizations. If membership in the Jewish
branch of the Knights of Pythias is added to that in other
exclusively Jewish fraternal organizations, 71 per cent of
the male membership may be considered as limited to
clubs identified with the Jewish group. For the French
Canadians whose social life is organized, 69 per cent of the
men's membership, and 86 per cent of the women's, is in
clubs confined to French Canadians exclusively or Catholics exclusively. For the Italians, 70 per cent of the men's
membership, and 83 per cent of the women's, is confined
in the same manner.

The Irish, the Germans, and the Old Americans show
greater freedom in their choice of social organizations.
Among the Irish, 52 per cent of the men's membership,
and 68 per cent of the women's, is confined to church or
religious-fraternal organizations. Among the Germans, 37
per cent of the men's membership, and 53 per cent of the
women's, is confined to clubs exclusively national. The
membership in church organizations raises this percentage slightly. It was more difficult to determine for the
Old Americans which organizations belonged exclusively
to their ethnic or religious group, since many clubs, although identified with either the Old American group or
with American Protestantism, are intended to serve all
qualified persons living in the community. The extent of
Old American membership in organizations, some of
which include only Old Americans, all of which include

only Protestants, may, however, be noted: 20 per cent of the membership of men, and 43 per cent of the membership of women, is confined to organizations connected with the church.

Thus, for the community as a whole, more than 53 per cent of the men's membership, and more than 68 per cent of the women's, is in clubs which do not include representatives of all ethnic groups in the community but are limited to people of one ethnic group or at most one religious group.

There are other allegiances, however, than those to ethnic and religious groups. Other interests bind people together, quite apart from ethnic heritage or religious affiliation. A Jew at one part of the day may be participating in a discussion within a Jewish organization concerning the particular problem of his group, but during another part of the day, as a business man or lawyer, he is concerned with problems not wholly Jewish. A French-Canadian woman may have started the day discussing family affairs in French over the breakfast table, after going to early Mass; but during the working day, as she serves behind the counter, she is concerned with the interests of her employer, her customers, and her fellow employees. Groups rising out of the common interests of the day tend to cut across ethnic and religious lines and form new units based on economic or occupational identification.

The business and professional men have many organizations which bring the persons of various ethnic and religious groups together. The Chittenden County Medical

Association, the Chamber of Commerce, the Chittenden County Bar Association, are a few examples. The extent, however, to which groups such as these counteract the influence of ethnic or religious groups depends upon the extent to which the various ethnic groups are represented in these professions. Thus, among the more highly specialized professions, such as law, there is relatively little intermingling of the groups; not because this is undesired but because there are among the lawyers few representatives of groups other than the Old American.

Closely connected with the immediate concerns of the business and professional groups are the organizations which bring together people who, though they may not have a common occupational interest, have a common class interest. Outstanding among these are the Rotary Club and the Lions Club. Both aim to bring together the leading representatives of each business and profession in the city for service to the community. The Rotary Club, however, invites to membership only one leading representative of each business, and since most leading business men are Old American, the tendency to be a club of one ethnic group as well as of one class is pronounced. Among the overwhelming majority of Old Americans and those of English or Scottish descent, there are to be found in this club only two or three of either French-Canadian or Irish descent, one Italian, one German. There are no Jews. The club has been criticized for the exclusiveness of its membership and for the fact that it has become a closed clique of business men who meet chiefly in order to exchange services with each other. As a result, the Lions Club, basing its membership on a similar but more inclusive plan, has taken the lead as the most active service club in the city. In 1934, although of its forty-eight members one half were of Old American stock, the other half included representatives of seven other nationalities — six Irishmen, three French Canadians, four Jews, two Scandinavians, three Germans, three Scots, and three Englishmen.

The two clubs have similar procedures at their meetings; both are concerned with the necessity of having a weekly speaker who will be brief so as to make it possible for the members to get back to business within an hour and a quarter. The problem in both groups is to get members to attend. The hale, hearty spirit and use of first names sometimes gives an impression of unreality, of a desire to achieve an intimacy which is lacking in the lives of most of the men. Topics for speakers at the luncheon meetings range from the weather, travel, social security, to the Oxford Group. One of the outstanding talks at the Rotary Club in 1935 was on Social Security, in which the speaker claimed that the price of such security would be the loss of the traditional American liberty and the ideals of individual effort responsible for the success of American business. The Lions, influenced by a talk given to the American Association of University Women, were more venturesome and permitted a Communist to explain Communism to them. While the talk to the Rotarians went without comment, except to get good headlines in the press, the talk before the Lions caused the Mayor to reprimand their organization in the newspaper.

An organization among women comparable to these is the Zonta Club, whose program and method of organization is similar to that of the Lions and the Rotarians. Of its twenty members, thirteen are of Old American or allied ethnic stocks, two are French-Canadian, four are Irish, and one is Jewish. The greatest value of the club would seem to be that it brings together women of recognized ability and leadership whether or not they have college degrees. It thus tends to be more inclusive than numerous other organizations which make up so much of the social life of many women, such as the Intercollegiate Club, the Smith College Club, and the University of Vermont Alumnae Club. In these, the main common bonds are likely to be class interests defined in terms of educational advantages.

Organizations such as the Rotarians, the Lions, the Zontas, together with the Elks, although basically social, are outstanding for their emphasis on service. Most of these organizations support the Elks in the "Kiddies' Luncheons" which are provided during the winter for all the poor children in the schools. The Rotarians send deserving boys to the Y. M. C. A. camp and subscribe to a milk fund for school children. The Zontas raise money for shoes for needy children, the Lions sponsor the State Music Festival and numerous other projects. All these organizations are eager for new "projects" of service to the community. The services are performed eagerly and, within limits, effectively; but insofar as their membership is of one class or dominated by one ethnic group, some of these services, at least, tend to reflect the interests of that class or group rather than the interest of the community as a whole. Their "civic" value, as the Lynds point out in discussing similar organizations in *Middletown,* is likely to be secondary:

> Certainly it is true that a wide gap exists between the activities of the civic clubs and the major maladjustments of which Middletown complains. In general, civic club members, like others, habitually regard these friction spots as inevitable accompaniments of life, and the city pursues its accustomed course with more or less creaking of the machinery in much the same manner as before the existence of the civic clubs. This situation presents few anomalies when it is realized that the clubs exist primarily as an adjunct to the business interests of their members and as a pleasant way of spending leisure; chiefly as a supplement to these interests and in regions where no enemies will be made or no ructions raised do the clubs become "civic." [1]

Clubs which still more definitely serve the social needs of the same business and professional group are those which furnish opportunities for recreation, such as the Burlington Country Club and the Lake Champlain Yacht Club, whose exclusiveness is assured by membership fees. The outstanding social club for this same group is the Ethan Allen Club, an outgrowth of a fire brigade by that name which, as the "white-collar" brigade of the early days of the town, consisting mainly of young men of the

[1] Robert S. Lynd and Helen Merrell Lynd, *Middletown* (New York: Harcourt, Brace and Company, 1929), p. 305.

Old American business class, was a rival of the working boys' brigade, consisting largely of Irish and some French-Canadian young men clerking in the stores or doing other varied jobs about town. Today, although the Old American group dominates the club, there is a considerable sprinkling of other nationalities, including a few Irish, French Canadians, and Jews. All these clubs concentrate primarily on purely social activities, such as dances and bridge parties. Although all these organizations are open to representatives of every ethnic group in the community, their dues make it impossible for any but a very small proportion of the newer ethnic groups to be members.

In marked contrast to the numerous organizations for the business and professional classes of the community are the few which meet the needs of the working class and the small business men. Whereas many of the men of the business class belonged to six, seven, or eight clubs, few of the working class belonged to more than two; and the average for the total working group was 0.7 clubs. The French-Canadian workers belonged to fewer organizations than did the Irish or German workers.

What the Chamber of Commerce and some of the other professional associations are to the business and professional men in the community, labor unions are to the working men, but the unions are not as strongly organized an expression of the workers as the Chamber of Commerce is of the business men. There are only eight active unions, including the recently organized textile union, and as one of their leaders explained, the unions are more apt to be bickering among themselves than working together. The weekly meetings are devoted to a discussion of labor conditions, of possibilities of jobs in various parts of the state, wage scales. In the carpenters' union, the present membership of which is 106, meetings draw some forty men; in the painters' union, members number sixty-five and meetings draw from thirty to thirty-five men. Some twenty years ago, when business was more flourishing in Burlington, the unions also flourished, serving not only as an educational center for the men but also as a social center for their wives.

Some of the men feel that if the women would only organize auxiliaries the unions could be a means of teaching the working-class people about just relationships between capital and labor. But the women have preferred to join fraternal or other organizations; only one of the unions ever had an auxiliary. One of the women of that group — the painters' auxiliary — explained that she met many women there whom she would never meet otherwise, and that French-Canadian, Irish, and Yankee women together learned about just wages and working conditions, but the contractor element within the group, who felt that the women were learning too much, caused the auxiliary to be disbanded.

Because of the correlation between ethnic groups and trades, organizations other than unions tend to reach a wider cross-section of the population. They are chiefly fraternal orders such as the Odd Fellows, the Eagles, the Elks, and the Woodmen, which appeal primarily to skilled artisans and white-collar workers. Here as nowhere else are to be found representatives of every ethnic group in the city. There is no organization for workers alone appealing to workers of every industry and every nationality, such as the International Workers Order; the nearest to this type of organization is the Fraternal Order of Eagles. Many ethnic groups in the community are represented, but even as the French Canadians are predominant in the working class, so they predominate in the Eagles, comprising about half the membership and holding many of the offices. These orders do not spend a great deal of time in listening to speakers. Occasionally they have a talk on community welfare, old age pensions, and the like, but in general they go through the formal matter of their business and ritual meeting and then join in a purely social time. Since these social times are the only ways of holding membership the tendency is to emphasize them more and more; the Eagles, for example, now have a beer license for their clubrooms, and this, as to many other clubs, is an important attraction as well as a valuable source of income.

Within recent years membership in these clubs has been dropping off considerably. Whereas the Eagles had a membership of 400 twenty years ago, they now have a membership of only sixty-five, and the average attendance at each semi-monthly meeting is between twenty and twenty-five. The Elks are a little more popular, but the membership has decreased from 600 members to 375, while their average attendance at monthly meetings is about forty members. The distinction between these two clubs in the rate of declining popularity reflects the economic level of their members. Two things operate to make the Eagles, appealing primarily to a lower economic level, lose members more rapidly: a decline in wages makes it impossible for the man who belongs to the Eagles to keep up his affiliation, since he is, on the whole, so close to the level at which he earns no more than his way; and prosperity among the workers does not help the Eagles because a very slight rise in salary may mean that some of the workers will shift their allegiance from the Eagles to the Elks, since the latter organization is thought to represent a slightly higher social and economic level.

In addition to these economic and class alliances which bring people together across ethnic and religious lines, there are other interests sufficiently universal to appeal to all people. The local art exhibits held at the Museum reveal an interest in painting among people of many walks of life in Burlington. It has been frequently pointed out that the art classes held under federal projects bring together a wider cross-section of Burlington than does almost any other activity. But the number in these classes is a small one, and the force of other social groupings is usually stronger than that of a common interest in art.

There is a widespread interest in the drama; drama groups are supported by the various churches, schools, and clubs. One such group, the Theatre Club, is considered a community organization, but its membership qualifications are not based on dramatic talent or interest in the drama so much as on certain qualifications of congeniality determined by the existing members. As a result, its understanding of what the community might like to see in the theatre is limited to a knowledge of what one social group wants to see.

Recognizing the importance of the drama in holding young people together, the French Canadians decided to organize a Theatre Guild under the guidance of one of their priests, primarily to hold together the young people of the parish. While it functioned, its performance was of good calibre, but as the priest in charge pointed out, when for their first perfomance he sent complimentary tickets to the Theatre Club of the city, not one member of the club responded by attendance. He named the three people of the Old American group who attended the performance and who are the only Old Americans to attend French-Canadian entertainments. He used the situation to illustrate that the social functions of each group in Burlington are attended only by that group, and that there is little exchange between the groups: when the Old Americans put on a play, it is attended by Old Americans; when the French Canadians do so, it is attended only by French Canadians; when the Irish put on a social function, it is attended largely by the Irish and other interested Catholics.

The community's interest in music, which might be another bond, has changed within recent years. Musical appreciation and attendance at professional concerts and recitals has not declined appreciably, but active participation in music making has decreased. In 1925 the *Burlington Free Press* was able to say in an editorial:

Burlington has long been recognized as the musical metropolis of northern New England. It is maintaining the proud distinction through various organized musical activities, including the Burlington Symphony Orchestra and the Burlington Symphony Society, instituted under the auspices of the Burlington Chamber of Commerce to serve as an auxiliary. The Burlington Symphony Orchestra was organized on December 20, 1922. . . . Even if our people did not appreciate good music, there would be ample ground for keeping up the traditions of Burlington as a musical center. The Burlington Philharmonic Society, organized on April 1, 1881, continued for nearly a quarter of a century to support famous music festivals for two or three days' duration. . . . The first Burlington Symphony Orchestra was established in 1910. In a similar way the work of the splendid choir and the orchestra which for years have augmented the organ at St. Joseph's Roman Catholic Church on stated occasions under the leadership of E. J. Beaupre has contributed to the fame of Burlington as a music center.

Gradually, however, a choral society which once flourished in the community has gone; and although the symphony orchestra is technically still in existence, it meets only for special occasions. A recent attempt to form another choral society under excellent leadership has met with only half-hearted support. Five church choirs still continue in existence, and Burlington is the center for the state music festival, at which an increasing number of school children throughout the state, with their bands and orchestras, meet; but for the general population, listening occasionally to a soloist of national repute or a string quartet imported from Boston or New York is the limit of musical activity.

A Community Concert Association brings some outstanding musicians to the community three times during the winter.

Since listening to music is in many respects more expensive than making it, the result of this change has been to limit any group musical activity to a small section of the population, predominantly Old American, able to afford concert tickets. The Athena Club, however, which strives to be a community organization, has a music department, and twice a month during the winter either cultivates music appreciation or listens to talks bearing on music. The program for the year is headed by the quotation: "See deep enough and you see musically, the heart of nature being everywhere music, if you can only reach it." Yet even this group appeals to a group economically, if not ethnically, predetermined.

A few organizations, such as the American Legion and the clubs organized about political affiliation, although they include French Canadians, Irishmen, and Old Americans, are usually identified with either one social class or one ethnic group predominantly. The American Legion, for instance, includes a cross-section of the population, but as one of its members remarked, "Its policies are largely determined by the more solid business men of the community."

There are other organizations which bring together in a more or less formal manner people sharing a common interest, but usually, because of high dues, they appeal to only one class of people in the community. One or two,

however, perhaps deserve special note as real agencies in
cutting across ethnic lines. One of these is the Athena
Club, frequently mentioned. Its efforts are expressed in its
motto, "The Union of All for the Good of All." With its
departments — Music, Art, Home Economics, Civics and
Health, and two departments of History and Literature, it
aims to reach the interests of a wide variety of women.
The characteristic programs of each department, however,
vary but little from year to year. Topics considered, for
instance, in the Afternoon History and Literature Department during one year were: "Autobiography of John Hays
Hammond," "Henry Wadsworth Longfellow," "Marquis
de Lafayette," "Snow Bound — by John G. Whittier."
The Evening History and Literature Department devoted
its major program as usual to some Shakespearian play.
The Art Department spent an evening each on such
topics as "Early Schools of Italian Art," "Leonardo da
Vinci," "Michelangelo," "Titian," "Rubens." The Civics
and Health Department devoted a meeting to such a
topic as "Beautifying the Home Grounds," "Moving Picture Symposium," "Vermont Laws."

Another important club with the same possibilities of
interesting a considerable cross-section of the people is the
Alliance Française, a social and cultural club aimed at
preserving interest in the French language and culture,
but the feeling has been that though this group certainly
should be one way of bringing French Canadians into
contact with Old Americans who are interested in keeping up the French language, the French Canadians have

not been very much interested either in being members of the club or in attending its French lectures. More and more, however, a few French Canadians attend its social gatherings, and both they and the Old Americans enjoy the social hour spent together, since both admit that if it were not for the opportunity thus provided, they would seldom, if ever, meet.

Another more recently organized society is the Delphians, with a three-year study-group program for women with both some money and some leisure. It consists of Protestant, Catholic, and Jewish women. In considering religious development in England during the time of the Tudors, these women have had to learn to continue studying together in spite of their widely different interpretations of that period. Some of them have not been able to learn this and have dropped out.

Interestingly, the University, which many people consider the center of the town's life, has little effect upon the social pattern. The student body has little to do with the town. Its life is set apart and self-contained. It has its dances, its clubs, its fraternities, and it seldom moves out of the circle these create. Similarly the professors and their wives either live in a small world of their own or, more usually, branch out into the Old American world, giving it additional numbers and the support of an intellectual justification for a feeling of superiority. "Certainly," said one man, with little realization of the implications of his remark, "there's no question but what, like the feller said, education is the handmaiden of the privileged classes. Those professors in the University don't do or say anything but what the people on the hill want them to. You don't see them coming down here to talk to me. I suppose, though, maybe they're right. I haven't got much to say to them. I don't know what makes the wheels go round, and the people on the hill think they do."

The University, it is true, sponsors lectures to which the whole community is invited, but the few that are devoted to world events are usually too theoretical in approach to appeal to any but the academically trained mind. No lecture in recent years has been on pressing economic issues facing America today. The lectures have usually been on such subjects as "Ancient Persian Rugs," "My Trip through China," "Old English Ballads." It is understandable that the French-Canadian mill worker, the German carpenter, the Irish storekeeper might prefer to go to the movies.

Beyond these organized attempts at union there are the innumerable informal groupings which make up the spontaneous social life of the city and which give a surface impression, at least, of warm interchange between all people. Particularly on the middle level of Burlington's social life, life energy aided by propinquity reaches beyond any set bounds. There are a number of personal friendships between Catholics, Protestants, and Jews; although some analytical people have declared that "there is always a difference in these friendships; there is always a whole world we cannot share, based on our religious differences." Within the last ten or fifteen years it has

been possible to find an Old American sitting down to the
same card table with some Irish and even a French Canadian. These are mostly neighborhood bridge clubs; and
though they are rarely, if ever, to be found at either the
top or the bottom of the society of Burlington, they are
looked upon by leaders of the newer ethnic groups of the
community as among the most hopeful signs of the coming together of people of different ethnic and religious
interests, of the beginnings of a new and richer social
life for Burlington.

Such, then, is the map of social life in Burlington. Economic barriers running horizontally, and religious and
ethnic barriers running vertically, divide the community
into small patches and set the pattern of its social life;
yet behind the barriers of ethnic and religious groups are
built similar organizations struggling with the same problems, having the same kind of programs. That religious
and ethnic organizations should play such an important
role in the community's life is partially due to the size
of Burlington, where each group is large enough to maintain distinct organizations long after the need upon which
they were originally based, namely, the protection of the
immigrant, has disappeared. The multiplicity of existing
organizations hinders the development of other organizations which would reach across these original barriers.
An editorial in the *Burlington Free Press* on this problem
as it confronts the average Vermont town can be applied
to Burlington itself. This editorial pointed out that as a
result of such multiplicity of organization, when the need

comes for a coöperative community enterprise, "no group can successfully compete for support strong enough to make it really effective."

Meanwhile, what becomes of the community itself? Each one of the competing groups will truthfully testify that one of its aims is to better its community. But the competition for time and membership among the groups, though it may not be recognized as inter-group competition, minimizes any attempt to contribute to civic progress.

Would it not be a worthwhile project for a council of the officers of the many organizations of a community to meet together and discuss the conflict that exists? It is too much to expect that many groups would voluntarily vote to disband. There is too much pressure on them from their state and national organizations. But this council of their representatives could coördinate some of their activity, with town progress in mind. It could plan, perhaps, one campaign each year for town betterment in which all the organizations worked together. It could draw up an agreement for somewhat less frequent meetings, and so arrange the calendar of meetings that all groups would gain in attendance and interest.

Certain it is that Vermont communities are receiving more harm than good from the mere number of organizations trying to benefit them. A large opportunity to secure organized loyalty is open to any town which succeeds in coördinating the efforts of these now conflicting groups.

To some extent the community desires that barriers be broken down. Some Old Americans, as well as members of other ethnic groups, wish they could meet other people. There are repeated references to the freedom of social intercourse achieved during the World War, when some of the traditional barriers were broken down and the community discovered interests which the barriers had prevented them from sharing. Since that time the only comparable example of the community being caught up in a general effort which transcended class and ethnic interest was the preparation for the N. R. A. parade, when once again people discovered similar interests among those whom they had never really known, from whom they had been separated by invisible barriers. In both the Catholic and the Protestant churches, prayers are continually offered for greater amity between the peoples of the earth, but when an attempt was made to put the principles of brotherhood between Catholic, Protestant, and Jew into practice within the community by getting a representative of each of these faiths to speak from one platform to a community gathering on Brotherhood Day, neither the Catholic priest nor any representative member of the flock could bring himself to participate, and so the whole thing failed.

The will to achieve amity lags far behind the wish that it exist. Even when gestures are made, their awkwardness reveals the lack of experience in handling community interrelationships, for the very tone of the community is one of tacit consent that it remain divided. When the Red Cross during the war period tried to combine women of various ethnic groups in a sewing project, the attempt failed because of attitudes of superiority and inferiority kept up by the women. The French-Canadian women were not comfortable among the others and withdrew to form the Ligue des Patriotes Franco-Americaines. As one of them explained, "They were more interested in having our French names on the list of workers to prove that it was a community enterprise than they were in having our presence." One Old American said: "Of course one may know people of other groups — but not too intimately, otherwise they're likely to forget their place." Another said: "Everything seems to be leveling us off these days. The War started it. Then the N. R. A., and now other government programs are trying to do still more of the same thing. There is too much leveling."

The organization of the social life of the city reflects the very important part ethnic and religious affiliations still play in determining the social life in an American community. When an individual must choose between membership in a club identified with his ethnic or religious group and membership in the same kind of club aiming to serve qualified members of all groups, his loyalty to his immediate group determines his choice. These organizations reflect the power of the group over the individual which was well expressed in an experience recounted by a Jewish woman. Once, she said, she was surprised and pleased when, making a casual remark to an Old American whom she had previously considered aloof and cold, she was rewarded with a response immediate and warm; yet she knew that although the invisible barriers of ethnic difference had thus fallen once, the next time the two women met they would be up again, since each woman would be aware of the eyes of the community on them; they would feel that both the Old American and the Jewish groups were watching to see how far they would go. As another woman explained it: "The town is too small and too large. It is so small that everybody knows when a person gets friendly with another, but it is not small enough for everybody to be friendly with everybody else." How, in practice, the group can exercise its taboo is indicated by the remark of an Old American business man: "When a newcomer arrives in town, we are not friendly immediately. We wait and see whom he picks out as his friends. If he picks out the wrong ones, he's finished as far as the right ones are concerned."

Faced with such silent but powerful opposition on the part of the group, it is small wonder that only the extraordinary individual is able to form deep friendships across ethnic, religious, or class lines, since by doing so he runs the risk of being held suspect by his own group. On the other hand, the person who yields to the pressure toward conformity finds compensation for the lack of mobility in the added sense of security and "belongingness" given him. In addition, the very fact that in a community of this size almost everyone knows, even though not intimately, everyone else, helps to maintain faith in the democratic tradition. If, however, the divisions which exist at present — economic, religious, or ethnic — should become more rigid, the vitality of the community's social life would decrease proportionately, and the individual's faith in America's traditional social mobility would die. If the community wishes to avoid this, it must somehow either continue to keep doors open between group and group, or, should this prove impossible, it must break down the barriers which have developed in its life.

CHAPTER IX

INTERMARRIAGE — A CRUCIAL TEST

WHEN a man and a girl wish to marry, in Burlington as in most of America, it is not as simple a
matter as it is in a more homogeneous country. The man
may be German, the girl French Canadian. He may be
Protestant, she Catholic. From every side they are subjected to pressures which make their decision difficult.
The girl's mother is likely to point out that the French
have never gotten along with the Germans. The priest
interferes: Is the man willing to turn Catholic? will he
guarantee that his children will be Catholics? Similar
pressures are brought to bear upon the man also, but the
emphases are more social than religious. The conflict of
two groups, two philosophies, works to keep them apart,
and, if they do marry, to separate them. Yet intermarriage
is perhaps the most significant single factor in building a
united people. Certainly it would be difficult for racial
prejudice to divide a community where a Yankee, for
example, knew his wife to be Italian, his children partly
Italian. The extent of intermarriage is thus a significant
indication of the extent to which ethnic allegiance as a
force for cleavage has been overcome.

It is difficult to ascertain the character of this process.
Marriage licenses give inadequate information because they
record only the birthplaces of the bride and groom and of
their parents. For the purpose of presenting a picture of

the extent of intermarriage in Burlington, information was secured in the preliminary survey of the city as to the ethnic origin of 3,677 householders whose wives were living; all those whose families had been three generations or more in this country were classed as Americans irrespective of their ethnic origin, and no distinction was made between those marriages among first-generation Americans which had occurred in this country and those which had occurred before the participants arrived. Thus the picture given here shows the extent of intermarriage in the community at a given moment, from the point of view of the men, without aiming to measure exactly the amount of fusion in such intermarriage and the trend in regard to intermarriage as did Bessie Bloom Wessel in *An Ethnic Survey of Woonsocket, Rhode Island.*[1]

In Burlington the amalgamating process, with the above qualifications, affects different groups to a different degree, some being more stable than others. Of the 180 Jewish householders in the community whose wives are living, only seven married outside of their group. French Canadians and Italians are next in their resistance to fusion, while the Irish and the Germans have experienced the fusion process more than any other peoples. Each group reveals a marked tendency to marry with third-generation Americans rather than with any others, and to marry with a wider range of nationalities in the second than in the first generation.

Of all the matings among 667 first- and second-genera-

[1] Chicago: University of Chicago Press, 1931.

tion French-Canadian householders, two thirds are marriages of French Canadian with French Canadian. Of the one third who have intermarried, 85 per cent have married third-generation Americans. To what extent this has been merely marriage with people of their own stock who had been here three generations or more is not known. Only 5 per cent of the total marriages are with groups other than French-Canadian or third-generation American. Among these, marriages with Irish are most numerous. The others represented are chiefly English Canadians, English, Germans, and Scots. The tendency toward marrying in a wider range increases in the second generation, 37 per cent of the second generation as compared with 18 per cent of the first being married to "Americans," and 7 per cent of the second as compared with 3 per cent of the first being married into other ethnic groups.

The same tendencies, although to a more marked degree, are to be seen among the Irish. Only one third of their marriages are within their own group. Of the remaining 66 per cent, however, almost two thirds are matings with Americans, many of whom are undoubtedly third-generation Americans of Irish stock. Ten per cent of 162 marriages classified are with French Canadians, 9 per cent with English Canadians. Other matings are with Germans, English, Italians, and Swiss. The proportion of intermarriages among the Germans is similar in extent and type to that of the Irish.

Intermarriage for the Italians is a practical necessity, since they are few in number. Twenty-four of sixty-eight householders have married outside their own group; the greatest number of these intermarriages are with Americans and French Canadians, but, notably, marriages with English, Irish, German, and English Canadians have also occurred.

The extent of intermarriage among Americans, including both Old Americans and people of other ethnic origin who have been here for three generations, is interesting. Although 20 per cent of 2,277 householders of this group married into a wider range of nationalities than did any other group, 80 per cent of them are married to other Americans of the third generation or more. This indicates, at least, how marked the tendency is for people to marry among those who are at home in the American environment, rather than among people of the first or second generation who may be of the same ethnic stock but who are less at home in this country.

In this connection it is significant that although the second generation of each group is inclined to be freer in the range of nationalities into which it marries, the greater proportion even of second-generation people marry into the same ethnic stocks as the parents. Thus a child of a French-Canadian and Irish intermarriage is more likely to marry a French Canadian or an Irishman than he is to marry an Italian or an Old American. Hence, intermarriages among the second generation, and perhaps even among the third generation, are in a large measure merely a reassortment of the same racial strains.

The forces which limit the extent of intermarriage in

the second as well as in the first generation are the result
of a complex of the factors that have been indicated in the
preceding chapters. An Old American is unlikely to marry
a French Canadian, not primarily because she is of different ethnic stock, but because she is likely to be on a
different economic level, to live in a less desirable neighborhood, to belong to a different church. From childhood
her difference from the Old American has been emphasized by education in a different school system. In short,
because of the rigidity of the social pattern, the French
Canadian and the Old American are not very likely to
meet.

The power of these factors is apparent in the attitude
of each group toward intermarriage. Only 25 per cent of
450 persons interviewed, representing all groups, insisted
that their people should marry only within their own
ethnic group, but an additional 11 per cent would permit
intermarriage only with similar ethnic stocks. Thus, more
than a third of all the people questioned are markedly
conservative in their attitude toward intermarriage. Only
a very few — 2 per cent of the entire number — took the
extremely liberal stand that one should be free to marry
anyone of any race or creed, but a majority, 62 per cent,
agreed that their people should be free to marry either
any white American or anyone within the white race.

The attitude toward intermarriage is not quite as liberal
as these figures would indicate, since when a check was
made by asking whether religious differences were of any
importance, a considerable number made immediate res-

ervations. For example, among those agreeing that one should be free to marry any white American, two thirds upon second thought qualified this statement by saying that marriage must be with persons of the same religious background. Those who were liberal enough to believe in marriage with anyone within the white race put less emphasis upon religious difference, but even the most generous excluded, on second thought, specific ethnic groups, especially Jews, Syrians, Italians, and Greeks. Thus it would appear that the first spontaneous liberal attitude toward intermarriage has many counterchecks when it comes to considering an actual situation. This was frequently expressed as follows: "I believe that one should be free to marry anyone whom one loves; but I personally would not care to marry outside of my own group. Few people who do are happy."

The several ethnic groups in the community showed marked differences of attitude toward intermarriage. The Jewish group exhibited extreme conservatism; fifty-three of the fifty-seven persons interviewed considered that Jews should marry only among their own people. The other four, however, held that Jews should be free to marry any white person or anyone of any race or creed; but this point of view was expressed only by those of the second generation. Some, recognizing the actual situation, said that though they believed Jews should be free to marry anyone, it was more satisfactory to marry only within their group. Others were concerned lest intermarriage mean complete assimilation. One danger, they pointed out, is that in such a marriage it is impossible for a Jew to preserve any of his religious customs or any of the dietary laws that mark him as a Jew. The other is that few persons are capable of transcending their cultural heritage sufficiently to appreciate another cultural tradition, or of making the allowances essential to success in such a marriage. This is especially evident when it comes to the question of children. Though they might be brought up as Christians they would find themselves identified with the Jews, even though Jewish customs and culture might be almost entirely foreign to them. The intensity of the feeling was perhaps most adequately expressed in such remarks as the following:

"Marriage in itself is a problem; aggravated by intermarriage it is doubly difficult. Each person in the marriage is unhappy underneath, each returns to his own, especially when near death; at high holidays there is always disagreement about religion; the children suffer." "The problem is in bringing up the children. They are neither here nor there. A child of mixed marriage is looked upon as if a crime had been committed. 'You're a mongrel' is the accusation thrown up to him." "Under prevailing conditions I wouldn't want my children to marry outside of the race, because Jewish people constantly inculcate in their children fear of the danger of assimilation."

The attitude of the French Canadians revealed both a loyalty to their group and a broadening point of view in the second and third generations. Forty per cent of 142

French Canadians expressing an opinion felt that they should marry either their own people or people of similar ethnic origin — 27 per cent wishing to have marriage exclusively within their own group, and 13 per cent willing to extend it to those of similar racial origin. Twenty-seven per cent, however, considered that the French should be free to marry any American, and 33 per cent, anyone within the white race; as would be expected, those who took the more liberal stand were less insistent that religion be identical for both parties in such a marriage. Forty-one per cent of the third generation, as compared with 25 per cent of the second and 18 per cent of the first, favored intermarriage with any white American, though there was practically no difference between the generations in attitude toward marrying anyone in the white race; and none took the very liberal stand that the French should be free to marry anyone of any race or creed.

The great conflict for the French Canadians is, as with other groups, not objection to actual biological fusion as such, so much as it is concern over certain cultural values. Intermarriage means a threat to the integrity of the ethnic group. The feeling prevails that if a French Canadian marries a person of a different communion, for example, he is lost to his church; and, because of its importance in preserving the integrity of the group, he is lost to his people. A French-Canadian priest pointed out that even if the Protestant member of the union is willing to become a Catholic, he is unlikely to be as wholehearted in his allegiance to the faith as the other partner. He is thus likely to sow, even though unconsciously, the seed of doubt in the mind of his child, who will continually be forced to choose between the values of his parents — one value that of the French-Canadian ethnic and religious group, the other that of the Protestant faith and the social philosophy that goes with it.

When such intermarriage does occur, the actual situation is met differently on two different social levels. Among the French-Canadian group in Lakeside, for example, the announcement that a girl contemplates marriage outside the Church is met by the community with great discussion and strong opposition, but if the girl is strong-willed enough to carry out her intention, when she returns to visit her family the community accepts her without thought of the problem which had earlier been of transcendent importance. A long tradition of submission to things as they are lies behind the words of one old Frenchman who explained, "After all, what's done is done."

Among those French Canadians who have graduated from this level into that of the great American middle class, however, such a simplicity of approach is not to be found. Their disapproval of a contemplated marriage outside the communion may be less vocal, but it is more lasting. One woman who contracted such a marriage found that she had lost all her old friends. The spirit of a principled middle class that refuses to recognize the needs that sometimes dominate people spoke in the words of a former friend, "One could forgive most things, but that she should give up her religion just to marry a man is unforgivable."

But marriage outside the ethnic group is opposed even if it be with someone of the same religion. In either case the integrity of the ethnic group is threatened. If a French Canadian marries a person of a different race though of the same religion he is lost to his people because in such a marriage the language, which is almost as strong a factor as religion in uniting the group, is likely to be dropped.

Many French Canadians, however, favored intermarriage with certain ethnic groups. They pointed out, for example, the advantages of marriage between French Canadians and Irish. As one French Canadian summed up the advantages of such a marriage, "The *savoir faire* of the French Canadian and the energetic drive of the Irish make a combination that can't be beat." A shrewd old mill worker qualified this statement by saying: "They will quarrel, though. It works out all right if it is an Irishman who marries a French girl; but if it is a French Canadian who marries an Irish girl, then he had better put on boxing gloves and watch out." Few comments indicate more clearly the differences in temperament of the two people. Yet most French Canadians, concerned with preserving their ethnic integrity, look upon intermarriage as a serious disintegrating force.

The attitude of the Old Americans toward intermarriage indicates a similar conservatism, based principally on pride of race. Although they were almost unanimous in their willingness to permit other races to intermarry, they did not believe so completely in intermarriage for themselves. By some the possibility of marrying a member of another group in Burlington was not even recognized. It is true that only 5 per cent of the Old Americans, as compared with 27 per cent of the French Canadians, agreed that they should marry only within their own group; but 29 per cent of the Old Americans, as against 13 per cent of the French Canadians, agreed that they should marry only people of similar ethnic stock. Hence, 34 per cent of the Old Americans, as compared with 40 per cent of the French Canadians, believed that their people should marry either within their own group or with a person of similar ethnic origin. The great majority, however, sixty-one of the ninety-eight persons interviewed, agreed that Old Americans should feel free to marry any American or anyone of the white race. Four were willing that Old Americans should feel free to marry anyone of any race or creed.

The Old Americans were concerned with differences of religion and were almost as conservative as any other group in this respect, but in contrast to the immigrant groups, they were greatly concerned with social and economic backgrounds. It was conceded, however, that when the social and economic backgrounds were similar "a little intermarriage would not be amiss."

The Italians were amazingly liberal in their point of view. True, eight of the thirty-nine persons interviewed agreed that Italians should marry only among their own people, but the remaining thirty-one were much more expansive. They did not confine intermarriage merely to any American — only three limited intermarriage to this group. Twenty-six considered that an Italian should be free to marry anyone within the white race; two went so far as to say that Italians should be free to marry anyone of any race or creed.

The Italians put less emphasis than other groups on the necessity of having the same religious background. They give the impression that they feel amalgamation necessary to the building of a great American people. This does not mean that they are not keenly aware of the difficulties of intermarriage; one illustration given of these difficulties was an instance of marriage of an Italian and a French Canadian, under which circumstances each person had to drop his native tongue and speak English, a language foreign to both. Language is such an integral part of the cultural values back of each person that difficulties arise in conveying to each other, in a tongue foreign to both, whole worlds of values. Yet there are cases in which these difficulties have been surmounted. As one Italian woman commented: "I think it is better if Italians marry only Italians, but they don't do that. If people are of good family, then intermarriage is all right. I didn't want anyone of my family to marry a Frenchman; but if an Italian girl got a French Canadian, as good a man as my daughter got, then it is all right."

The attitude of the Germans and the Irish toward intermarriage was very similar, the Irish being a little more conservative than the Germans. Both were more liberal than any other groups. Twenty-three (or 28 per cent) of the eighty-one Irish persons interviewed, as compared with ten (or 30 per cent) of the thirty-three Germans interviewed, agreed that their people should be free to marry any American; forty-six (or 57 per cent) of the Irish, as against twenty-two (or 67 per cent) of the Germans, agreed that they should marry anyone within the white race. Both took points of view fairly similar to that of the Old Americans, who said that the chief difficulties in intermarriage were due first to differences in the religious background, and second to differences in social and cultural traditions. A remark frequently made by both, however, was that "intermarriage is all right as long as both families are respectable and honorable."

Such a remark, conventionally evasive, probably conceals a recognition of real difficulties. For, as one cautious German pointed out, the problems of intermarriage are real and important, and not easily solved. "I don't think we're ready for too much intermarriage yet. I think we've in many respects been too hasty in bringing people together. The whole difficulty with modern marriage has been that when a man wants to marry his primary consideration is whether or not he likes the girl. That's important. But just as important is the cultural tradition which, if he marries outside it, will separate him and his wife on many issues. I can see the difference in my brother's marriage and mine. I married a German girl. He married a Yankee. We both have difficulties. But whenever a troublesome situation arises, my wife and I can meet it from the same point of view, can measure it in terms of the same values; while he and his wife have to approach it from two different angles, and it is often difficult for them to get together."

At a slow and uneven rate, therefore, the complicated process of building a united people through intermarriage goes on in Burlington. Ethnic and cultural distinctions play important roles in preserving the separateness of groups, but economic, social, and religious differences are the primary factors in retarding the blending of peoples. Offsetting these are the forces of common interest that rise out of a common American environment. Where intermarriages occur, they still take place largely among people sharing a common religious belief as well as common social status. The children of an intermarriage are usually thrown back upon one or the other of the ethnic groups of which their parents are representatives, and in the second generation, the intermarriages are usually a reassortment of the first ethnic strains within a common cultural unit, such as religion, rather than a branching out beyond it.

In the past this group-consciousness has been a force in maintaining a stable and established way of life, giving to each individual a feeling of "belonging" to a small group. Valuable, however, as it has been during the period when the rest of America was developing with disorganizing rapidity, there is a possibility that it may show another side of its character in the future. Beneath the pressure of social change in the world as a whole, it may well be that this force will be used to divide the community as it has some European nations. Intermarriage so far has not been sufficiently frequent to preclude such an eventuality.

CHAPTER X

THE COMMUNITY AND ITS CIVIC LIFE

THE people of any community form innumerable groups which divide, unite, and re-form to meet various needs or specific interests, but above and beyond these groupings — social, economic, and religious — there are certain concerns common to all. These may be viewed differently according to the level on which the individual approaches them, but everyone in the community is essentially interested in them; they are the general forces and factors that determine for each individual the extent to which his activities shall be regulated in deference to some common purpose. The political and charitable activities of the community are here presented as a means of showing how far a sense of common responsibility exists on the part of the citizens.

PARTICIPATION IN GOVERNMENT

Politically, Burlington shares a common faith in the American ideal of a democratic government. Under this system, it believes, each individual is free to plan and mold his own life; each has a voice in the policies of the government. Yet the citizens of Burlington fear that this way of life which has been considered an expression of the highest ideals of mankind is threatened; the newspapers and radio remind them that in some parts of the world it is no longer valued and has been superseded by dictatorships of one form or another. Resolved that "these things must not happen here," the people are not sure how to avoid them. In an attempt to keep out these foreign dangers, they have, in many sections of America, permitted a restriction of the very civil liberties which they wish to protect. Charles Beard, for example, has pointed out that in our anxiety to reject anything labeled "un-American" we may slip into an American brand of Fascism. One first step in that direction, he felt, can be seen in the rise of such policies as the compulsory "Teachers' Oath." As one Burlington minister pointed out: "We are all worried about Fascism, but we think that it will only come through the present policies of the Democratic party. We don't realize that it is quite as likely to come through the Republican party. If we were only willing to see that too, we might prevent dictatorship."

Newspaper articles and editorials and political speeches do little to clarify the feeling of the public in regard to Fascism and Communism. Lumped together under the one word "un-American," they are summarily rejected, and the concepts which they embody are never explained. The newspapers content themselves with crying "Wolf" at every unliked policy of the opposition. In the *Burlington Free Press,* a Republican paper, for example, on one day the "Democrats are seen marching into Collectivism unaware of it," while on another day they are said to show an "approach to Fascism." The implication is that by electing the Republican candidate one can avoid both these dangers.

Because of this uneasiness about the possible threat to the democratic ideals of the country, the average citizen is suspicious of any marked social change. In time of grave distress, it is true, he looks for something to help him; thus, both working class and business class in Burlington were glad of government intervention during the early part of the depression; but with the pickup in business of more recent years, business men are concerned with shaking off government interference; they are troubled by the corporation taxes, unemployment insurance, and other possible social legislation that may add one more burden to the overburdened little business man, which is every business man in Burlington. Although they express their fear of this interference as a fear of dictatorship, some feel they might accept a dictator who was of their own kind, a Republican with the interests of their class at heart.

The working people, on the other hand, although generally convinced that their lot will not be improved without some government help, are very conservative in their stand. Two leaders among the working men, one a Yankee, the other a French Canadian, expressed the desires of the working class as follows: "There will have to be change to catch up with changing times. There has to be a limit of hours of work in order that everybody can work, and a minimum wage so that people won't starve." "What we want is a saving wage, not just a living wage. That, however, I feel sure, can be gotten within the two-major-party system as we now have it. Labor will never have a political party of its own." A few, however, are becoming a little impatient with the slowness with which the improvement of their lot comes. As one Italian explained, "I don't really believe in dictators. They are more apt to be bad than good. But there is no doubt about it that somebody like that gets a few things done, and we need to get things done."

Much of this conservatism is based on the personal relationships still possible in Burlington between employer and employee and on the appreciation of each other's problems which results. None of the workmen interviewed ever questioned the right of an employer to make profits; they were all proud to be able to say that there were no Communists among the workers in Burlington. Such an attitude is largely strengthened by the influence of the Catholic Church, which emphasizes the anti-religious element of Communism and of some forms of Fascism; at least a sermon preached on the menace of Fascism and Communism emphasized the dangers in such countries as Russia, Germany, Spain, and Mexico, where religious freedom is limited, though whether the kind of Fascism existing in Italy would be more acceptable was not made clear. As a whole, however, the political concerns of the people of the community do not focus on such issues except as they enter on the outer periphery of their political life, or as the terms "Communism" and "Fascism" may be used to condemn the political platform of one dominant party or the other; Burlington discusses and votes rather in terms of a struggle between states' rights and a strong central government, or in terms of individual independence and social inter-dependence.

One of the most hotly debated issues in recent times was the question of building a parkway along the top of the Green Mountains which in time would connect with a large national parkway, the whole plan to be financed by the Federal government. Vermont rejected the project. For many persons, objection to it was based on the fear that such a highway would bring undesirable tourists into the state and despoil the mountains for mountain lovers, but to others, the issue was whether or not, by permitting such a highway, Vermont should expose itself further to the influences from outside. When, immediately following this episode, the Federal government offered to pur-chase marginal lands, determined by a Vermont commit-tee, on which a state reserve could be built, Vermont's refusal was an even more definite indication that the state does not want Federal interference. As the *Burlington Free Press* commented, "The Legislature looked at the whole matter as the work of Dr. Tugwell or the Devil and voted 'No'."

In such highly independent terms does Vermont, and Burlington as a part of it, express its desire to be left alone to work out its destiny and preserve an undisturbed order of things. Burlingtonians, perhaps because of urban influ-ences, have shown more concern than the inhabitants of many other parts of the state with general problems of social change and adjustment. In the winter of 1933-34 during the worst part of the depression, there was a public forum in Burlington, which, though it dealt almost exclusively with international problems rather than with national or local issues, did help the people to see their problems in a larger light and to realize that the whole world was concerned with issues in which Burlington, whether it liked it or not, was inevitably entangled.

An expression of doubt as to whether or not the old order is doing all that it might is to be found in the development of a political conflict between the young people and the older of the community, but the Young Republicans and Young Democrats, although they may have new ideas, are interested more in changing control within the party than in changing fundamental policies. The Young Republicans did not get very far with their organization when one of the older members of the party assured them that they really had a good deal of influence in the party as it was, and that they would have less by splitting off; furthermore, they would then have neither the funds nor the rooms which the Old Republicans were willing to supply them. When in addition the plea was made that at a time when the country was in such a critical condition, Republicans should not be divided among themselves, no young man or woman rose to uphold any ideals for America differing from those of the old guard. The speech of the Old Republican had its effect and the Young stayed within the fold.

This lack of consciousness of any serious issues at stake characterizes even the students of the University of Vermont. There are no student clubs, for example, interested in pressing social issues, although one concentrates on studying present-day diplomatic relations. The absence of any social science department is probably a factor in the conservatism of these young people, but another most important force for it is to be found in the influence of the Reserve Officers' Training Corps and compulsory military training. Sufficient pressure is put to bear upon possible leaders of the student body, and especially on the editor of the student paper, so that any speculation on social issues is discouraged. The student paper has not only condemned such a movement as the Veterans of Future Wars; it has also, under orders, some students and professors contend, from the administration and the military department, refused to print letters or news stories praising any general peace movement. The student body does not participate in the peace demonstrations which have occurred in practically all the colleges in the country in recent years.

Local issues are much more interesting to the population: whether or not the community should have a filtering plant for its water supply, or a municipal electrical plant; or should make zoning a part of a community program; whether or not Church Street should have ornamental lights; whether trees should be cut down on lower Pearl Street so as to widen the street for traffic. An important issue which has arisen when the city has been hard-pressed for finances has been that of taxing fraternity houses.

Concerning all these questions, Burlington citizens are

expected to show their interest and active concern. A recent editorial in the *Burlington Free Press* stressed the first essential of good government as the selection of good men and women to hold office. Another editorial claimed that "it is the voter who stays away from the polls and so is not represented on election day who makes bad government possible. If every Vermonter would go to the polls and vote his honest convictions at each election, and then support his vote by his actions, there would be much better government in this country." There is a general feeling, however, that on many issues the community is apathetic. On the question of annulling the prohibition amendment, the local newspapers pointed out that not more than 25 per cent of the voters were sufficiently interested to go to the polls. Nevertheless, there seems to be a fairly high sense of civic responsibility toward voting. Certainly to the question, "How often do you vote on local, state, and national issues?" the Old Americans and the Irish especially gave answers which indicate that they still take the privileges seriously — the one group in opposition to the other. Ninety-five per cent of the Irish questioned, and 86 per cent of the Old Americans, claimed that they always vote on local, state, and national questions. Germans and Jews came next, with 79 per cent and 78 per cent respectively; but among the French Canadians and the Italians, less than half — 48 per cent of the former and 45 per cent of the latter — said they voted at each election. A high percentage, 33 per cent and 38 per cent of these groups respectively, said they never vote. This was more true of the women than of the men.

When a political struggle is going on which captures the attention of the community as a whole, no one group is more active than another. The voting records of the city election of March, 1933 show that the wards of the melting pot and the "pure" wards were represented at the polls in comparable proportions — 76 to 77 per cent of the taxpayers in all the wards except the fifth showing up at the polls. In the national elections of 1932 some 82 to 96 per cent of the taxpayers in each ward voted. The fact that Wards 1 and 6 led all others in representation at that time may indicate a greater interest on the part of the longer established peoples in the community in national questions, just as the large percentage of representation from the "immigrant wards" in the city elections of the following year may indicate a proportionally greater interest on the part of the newer peoples in local questions.

As a whole, however, the way one votes is largely a traditional matter. The community lines up into two camps, Republican and Democratic, with the Old Americans the champions of the Republican party, the Irish the champions of the Democratic. Members of both groups not in the camp traditional to their kind feel it necessary to explain the reasons. The peoples of the other groups fluctuate between the Republican and the Democratic parties according to the influences at work at the time.

Chance or tradition, therefore, rather than analysis of policies, determines the affiliation with the political party.

Among the Old Americans, for example, the reasons given for their choice of party were expressed as follows: — "My father and grandfather were Republican before me and I am a Republican too." "I vote independently, but my affiliations are those of the Republican party because the Republican national policy is the best for the country." "My family tree is Republican." "What I want is fine character in a candidate, and it is usually to be found in the Republican party." "I am a Republican. It was decided for me by Mr. Abraham Lincoln." The strength of this tradition is apparent even in regard to state elections. At the present time it is felt that never has the Republican party had fewer able men to run for the office of Governor than at present. A group of women were to be heard bemoaning that fact and at the same time commenting on what an admirable man the Democratic candidate was. When a visitor in the group innocently commented that she hoped, then, that he would be elected Governor, there was momentary consternation. The women looked at each other and one finally explained, "Oh, but you see, we can't do that. After all, he is a Democrat."

The Irish, on the other hand, look upon themselves as the champions of the newer elements. They refer frequently to the times in American history when efforts were made to restrict the privileges of immigrants. The Irish comments are always related to the fact that they as a group stood for the Democratic party when it represented the rise of the immigrants against the "American policy" of the period. They have gradually won over to the Democratic ranks many of the French Canadians who in the early days used to vote Republican chiefly because their Old American employers told them to do so, but who, as one Old American admitted, "if left to themselves, would all be Democrats." Thus today the allegiance to political party, which at one time combined French Canadian and Yankee against Irishman, is now more and more an alignment of newer versus older Americans. This fact tends to increase the force of the demarcations already established along economic, cultural, and religious lines between these two main groups in the community.

In Burlington, as elsewhere, a factor in determining the way in which some people vote is bribery or coercion. This may take such mild forms as giving advice to one's workmen, as in the mills, where the French Canadians sometimes follow the ideas of their employer as to how they should vote. It may take the more common form of openly buying the vote with a small tip, which used to be a cigar or fifty cents but which, since the repeal of the prohibition amendment, has become a couple of drinks. Or it may even take the form common in larger cities, where ward "bosses" control blocs of votes. There are no big political bosses in Burlington as yet, but there are influential men who do control the votes of a number of persons who rent their houses or are under obligation to them in some other way. One man, for example, is conceded to control 128 votes on a purely mercenary basis; another is said to control practically the entire voting power of a small ethnic group. It is said that some groups seem to be more susceptible to bribery than others, but no group is entirely free from it. Some are merely at the dispensing, rather than at the receiving, end of the process.

Once the people of the community have voted, for all the various reasons listed above, the great majority then sit back and indulge in no political activity, other than discussion, for the rest of the year. Their elected representatives then carry on for them.

Every ethnic group in the community has some representatives among the group entrusted with the responsibility of governing the city, either holding top public positions, or lesser ones, or being employed by the city. From the time Burlington was organized as a city in 1865 until the present, every mayor except one has been of Old American or of allied ethnic stock. In 1903, for the first time, an Irishman broke the long line of Old Americans to become mayor; since that time he has been reëlected six times, but no other member of one of the newer groups has succeeded in breaking in.

This election of an Irish mayor in 1903 also marked another change, in that for the first time the larger proportion of the population voted the Democratic instead of the Republican ticket. Prior to the election of 1903, only three of the seventeen men who had been mayors of Burlington since 1865 had belonged to the Democratic party, and these mayors had held the position for only six out of the thirty-eight years. Since the 1903 election, two of the seven men who have been mayors have belonged to the Democratic party, and, in contrast to the earlier representatives of their party, have held the position for twenty-two of the thirty-three years.

Although the mass vote of the Democrats now carries great weight in the election of the mayor, it has little influence on the election of aldermen. In 1935, when the majority vote of the community was conceded to be Democratic, nine of the twelve aldermen elected were identified with the Republican party. Seldom is a Democrat elected from any ward other than 3 or 4. That a change in the districting of the wards might lead to a somewhat different representation on the Board of Aldermen is indicated by the remark of one of the city officials who pointed out that when, in a general election, Ward 4 decides to go strongly Democratic, its voting strength is sufficient to ensure that the Republican vote of the entire city will be overridden.

The ethnic distribution of the aldermen is similarly disproportionate. Of the twelve members in 1935, six were of Old American stock, three were Irish, two were French-Canadian, and one was Jewish.

The central group in control of city affairs, namely, the Mayor, the Chairman of the Board of Aldermen, and the City Treasurer, has always been in the hands of the Republican party, with at least two of the posts always filled by Republican representatives of the Old American group. Hence, though the Democrats have frequently expressed their majority power by voting for a Democrat as mayor, they have never as a party had control of city affairs. On the School Board, also, the Old Americans retain their influence. In 1935 there were four Old Americans; one German, second-generation; and one French Canadian, third-generation.

Among the twenty-five city officers, the Old Americans have the largest representation. Although the Irish are well represented, there are only two or three French Canadians and one Jew. It is only when one reaches the list of lesser officials in public office that one finds a larger representation of the newer ethnic groups. This is particularly true of the French Canadians, although they are not in positions of authority. Of the thirty men on the police force in 1934, for example, twelve were French Canadians, eleven were Irish, including the Chief of Police, four were Old Americans, one was French, one Italian, and one Jewish. Of the forty-one men in the fire department in 1934, twenty were of French-Canadian stock, nine were Irish, seven were Old American, including the Fire Chief, one was German, two French, one Polish, and one Scottish. Thus, although all of the ethnic groups of the community are represented in city affairs to some extent, the leading positions of trust and responsibility are still largely held by Old Americans.

Because of the disproportionate representation of some of the ethnic groups in public life, and especially of the French-Canadian group, the question was asked of members of each group: "Have you or any of your friends experienced prejudice in running for, or holding, public office?" In each group the majority did not consider that such prejudice played much part, if any, in their attempts to gain public office. Most of the Irish, however, admitted that when Al Smith ran for President they were forced to realize that such prejudice did exist, although on a religious rather than on a nationality basis. At that time, the coming to life in this very community of the Ku-Klux Klan proved to them that the city was not immune from such religious prejudice toward their holding office.

More than any group, the Jews considered that prejudice hindered their holding public office, and some cited situations that had occurred in this city as examples of this prejudice. More than half of these considered that the keenest opposition to their holding public office came from the Old American group. The French Canadians and the Italians pointed out that representatives of their people ran for office so seldom in competition with representatives of more dominant groups that the existence of such prejudice had seldom been tested. The Old Americans were freer than any group from feeling any prejudice in running for public office, although some admitted strong competition from the Irish.

Members of each newer ethnic group consider that often jealousy within the group, as well as prejudice without, is responsible for their lack of representation in public life. The French Canadians, particularly, say that instead of standing together and helping one of their members to attain public office, as they believe the Irish do, they jealously watch each other's advancement and frequently hold a member down if he seems to be making too rapid progress beyond the group. Rather than give power to one of their own members or to their keenest rivals, the Irish, they have frequently preferred to give it to one of the Old Americans of the Republican party whom many of them still filially regard as impartial leaders to be trusted with the affairs of the community as a whole. In the same way the Irish are less unified than they appear. If they feel that their man is getting too far ahead of them, they will support a Yankee, whom they do not suspect of ulterior motives to the same extent that they tend to suspect one of their own people who may be "getting beyond himself."

It is for these reasons that the Old Americans have usually held the more responsible positions in the community's politics. They have been looked upon as having wide, impersonal, and very real public interest; whereas the other groups, it is thought, tend more to have petty political interests.

The major part of the city government is in the hands of the Mayor and the Board of Aldermen. Elected from each ward, these aldermen represent wide differences in outlook; consequently every issue, whether large or small, is held up by the arguing and bickering between the various members. Inexperienced in matters of government, many of the newer members are inclined to trust the judgment of the aldermen whose education and business knowledge seem greater than their own; and in addition, of course, when issues are up which concern special interests in the community, they are advised by these interests how best to vote. Actual opportunities for making money through political graft, however, are small in a city the size of Burlington, though occasionally an interested outside business concern has been known to offer certain sums of money to aldermen who have been uncertain how to vote. On the whole, it is accepted that people do not go into politics for purely altruistic reasons, that as in any other part of America they go into it largely for what they can get out of it. The business advantage of getting his name before the public has determined many a business man to take part in political affairs, but political graft is so much in the American tradition that the average citizen of Burlington takes it for granted.

As compared with other New England communities of its size, Burlington is no better and no worse in its management of municipal affairs, and beneath all the bickering and wide differences of outlook there is one concern upon which all members of the Board of Aldermen are united — that is, Burlington. An amusing illustration of this unanimity of aim is afforded by an account of their action when the fire chief petitioned the aldermen for a new car. There was at first considerable discussion about whether the budget permitted his having a new car or whether he might not have to wait until the beginning of the next fiscal year. The problem seemed insoluble even though he pointed out that his car had gone 90,000 miles, that it was beyond repair, that he had to drive in other men's cars or go to fires on foot. At last, however, he hit upon an argument which settled the point. He rose from his seat in the audience and explained that he didn't think he had been unduly extravagant, having had only three cars in thirty-three years, but aside from that, the urgent reason for his having a new car was that within two weeks, as President of the New England Fire Chiefs, he was to attend a meeting in Hartford, Connecticut.

"Gentlemen," he said, "do you want me to go to this meeting, representing Vermont, in a tumble-down car that may break down in the middle of Hartford?" A hush fell over all the group present; one or two aldermen put forth a few feeble efforts at further discussion to prove a certain sense of independence, but the actual matter was closed. The fire chief got his car.

The major criticism which the community makes of its government is that the men who now go into politics are no longer of the high caliber of their predecessors. In the main, it is said that the persons who enter politics today are less likely to have the same high ideals of public service which, it is felt, characterized the officeholder of an earlier day. The Old Americans, in general identified with the Republican party, are, according to one leading representative of the newer peoples, "tired of running affairs but unwilling to give up their power either to their own people of the younger generation or to any different people." Some Old Americans, on the other hand, say that they are fearful of relinquishing their authority, and point to the political corruption in cities like New York, Boston, and Chicago, which they feel is largely due to yielding too much authority to peoples new to the ways of democracy. Yet the tendency among the Old Americans in Burlington, as among the established groups in any community, is to be the power behind the scenes. More and more they let personally selected delegates exercise power in politics, but they keep a controlling hand over them lest they foster a movement alien to the Old American interpretation of what would be good for the community. Though they thus prevent the newer groups from getting any real power, sometimes the type of representative the Old Americans choose to be their professional politician is the type who more than any other may lead the community into strange fields. The Shad Ladue of Sinclair Lewis' "It Can't Happen Here," which made many Old Americans shiver, is not necessarily to be found among the ranks of the newer peoples of the working class; some Burlingtonians think they can see his counterpart in one of the Old American-supported leaders of the local Republican party.

If the newer peoples become disappointed in the leadership of the Old Americans and have no opportunity to develop a leadership of their own with real power, they may turn from the Old Americans in much the way described by Herman Feldman in his *Racial Factors in American Industry,* and "become particularly susceptible to the mass appeal of the demagogue who praises their virtues and talks to them on terms of equality. The disparaged groups become fit subjects for political moves by which they are led to cast their balance of power in favor of predatory political machines." [1] On the other hand, because of the

[1] Page 183.

great desire to preserve things as they are, a tendency toward a form of government alien to American ideals may develop in another way. Before the pressure of social change which may be too rapid for Burlington to assimilate, there may be a marked reaction in the name of some emotionally charged slogan such as "Americanism," "Saving the Constitution," or "Escaping the threat of Communism," into a form of government not markedly different from what we know today as Fascism. In Germany and other European countries many people have sacrificed their beliefs in a changing order that they might preserve something which they were led to believe was the Democratic State, only to find themselves in the Fascist State.

Neither of these eventualities need result. The community of Burlington may align itself with a social change which will preserve the democratic principles which have become lost or blurred in the pressure politics of powerful groups. It will not do this, however, if the changes that come, come too fast or are made to appear to be coming too fast by those whose special interest it is to see that there is no change. If the community were freed of this kind of pressure, the ideal of democracy might gain fresh vitality which would lead to the discovery of expanding possibilities for the individual and the community.

Thus, although Burlington reacts against such words as Fascism and Communism, it is not unaffected by the forces at work in the world.

CARE OF THE NEEDY

There is no more obvious common concern for all members of a community than that of helping their fellow citizens who are in need; in the face of dire want one would expect the differences of race and creed to disappear. The care of the poor, of the sick, of the delinquent, is a problem which should command the interest, if not the activity, of every member of the community. The extent to which these problems are shared is therefore an index of the community spirit.

Certainly there is no lack of charitable giving in Burlington. When attempting to ascertain how those in need are helped, one is confronted with a host of societies, organizations, institutions, and individuals, all concerned in whole or in part with helping the unfortunate. Giving alms to the poor is an accepted Christian duty, and provides special opportunity for serving those who are peculiarly God's children.

This giving of help in general sets the limits to social service work in the community. There is, as yet, little attempt to consider the bases of poverty and need and to work toward a society in which the poor shall not be so overwhelmingly with us. The concern in regard to poverty is still chiefly with two conflicting ideas of how charitable work shall be administered. The old idea of person-to-person assistance given in the name of Christian charity is opposed to the more modern conception of organized social work. The sentiment of the public in Burlington still leans toward emphasis on the former. Champions of organized social work may point out that unorganized individual charity is inefficient and in some ways harmful; they may say that it depends upon an almost accidental coming together of the persons in need and those capable of meeting that need; that the evaluation of need is based on no standard other than that of the individual "Lady Bountiful," whose charitable enthusiasm is likely to reach a peak at Thanksgiving and Christmas and to dwindle thereafter, leaving the poor neglected. But the defenders of person-to-person giving are even more critical of organized social work. The latter is, they contend, an unsympathetic, mechanistic means of doing what should be done by good neighbors without "overhead costs"; furthermore, it is likely to take care of the "unworthy" as well as the "worthy" poor; it shows a tendency to question the Biblical dictum that the poor are always with us; and it is depriving some people of the satisfaction to be derived from giving themselves. Thus, although thousands of dollars are spent annually for helping those in need, charitable activities are not coördinated into a unified program. Each group or social organization concerned with helping the needy is concerned with helping in its own way; furthermore, each organization tends to see its function as that of supplementing the general relief work of the city charity department, rather than in terms of qualitative or experimental work which might ultimately prove of greater social value.

A number of organizations, such as the Masons, the

Rotary Club, the Eagles, the Elks, and the Saint-Jean-Baptiste Society, do supplementary work which takes the form of helping the families of their members who are in difficulties because of sickness or unemployment. Other organizations concentrate their activity on supplying the underprivileged of the general community with the material needs for which provision is already made in the city ordinances in regard to the Charity Department. Thus, for example, although provision is made in a city ordinance for supplying needy school children with shoes, the St. Anne's Societies of the Catholic churches, the Zonta Club, some of the Parent-Teacher Associations of the schools, and numerous small social clubs concentrate on this single aspect of social service, in some cases to the exclusion of all others. The inadequacy of the work done is forgotten in the glow of satisfaction which comes from the realization that one is "doing some good," yet splendid as some of these projects are as an expression of community coöperative endeavor, the emphasis on "doing good" without making a realistic evaluation of the good done results inevitably in mere palliative patchwork.

A further consequence of the present method of giving aid is favoritism. In a community where so much social work is done by volunteers or poorly paid trained workers, the traditional tendency to classify the poor as deserving or undeserving is inevitable. Moral evaluations in regard to the worthiness of a case vary from person to person, and are seldom subjected to any scientific investigation. "Uncoöperative" is a favorite word among all those meting out charity, and it usually means that the recipient of aid is not showing the proper Christian humility and gratitude, or is unwilling to accept the dictates, often arbitrary, of the person who is helping. One woman was discovered by one of the agencies in town to be, with her four children, perilously close to starvation. She and her children had been on the list of the public charities, but when her husband, who had left them, had been discovered in a near-by state where he was working, and had agreed to take the children and care for them, the woman had refused to give them up. It had then been decided that she was uncooperative, and her name had been struck from the Charity Department's list of those considered "worthy" of help.

Any number of similar instances could be listed where the poor, because they are "uncoöperative," are refused assistance. In many cases these persons then merely transfer their importunities for assistance to other agencies. Families have been known to be members of St. Joseph's parish at one time, the Cathedral parish at another, the Baptist Church next, according to the amount of aid that these organizations will give them, while at the same time they may petition any number of other agencies and individuals throughout the city. The demoralization of character which this fact expresses is not considered to be in any way due to the failure of the agency itself, or of the coöperation between the agencies, or ultimately of the system in which some individuals must learn to beg from door to door.

In spite of these limitations, which some people recognize, the community as a whole is not yet ready to accept the reforms, limited though they might be, which might result from greater coördination of charitable work and consequent redefinition of the function of the private agency. A characteristic attitude toward centralized social service was evident when the Federal government first offered to aid the various states in handling their relief problems. Vermont's answer was, "Vermont can take care of its own." Admirable as this stand may be under many circumstances, by 1936 Vermont had had to accept $62,-000,000 from the Federal government to handle its relief problem. This includes loans of all kinds, support of Civilian Conservation Corps camps, and outright grants. But faith in the principle of taking care of one's own still persists to a considerable extent. When the question was asked in Burlington whether each ethnic group should take care of its own, 46 per cent of those interviewed believed that the group should assume this responsibility, 6 per cent were uncertain, and 48 per cent disagreed.

Among those who agreed, the attitude taken is best expressed in the comments by two Old Americans: "Each group should take care of its own if it is able, just as the Jews do." "Each group should take care of its own until they are willing to be truly American." Interestingly enough, the two groups which were most completely in agreement with the idea were the French Canadians, who receive more aid from general public agencies than any other group, and the Jews, who, more than any other group, do take care of their own poor. The French-Canadian point of view, however, represented to some extent wishful thinking: "It would be nice if we could do this"; while the Jewish agreement was based on the feeling that whether desirable or not in the abstract sense, "Jews must take care of their own because those in need must be protected against possible discrimination in any general private or public agency."

Persons in every group, however, admitted the inability of each group to take care of its needy members, even in the best of times. Among the 48 per cent who disagreed with the advisability of doing so, many pointed out that putting emphasis upon care of the needy by their own group tended to preserve separatism. Interestingly enough, the Jews expressed this better than any other people: "Caring for those in need should be a community problem, not a problem for each group. The fact that the Jews more than any other group take care of their own gives many Gentiles the wrong impression that all Jews are rich." "It should be a community problem. Each group is a part of the community, and when each cares for its own, it not only encourages separatism but breeds race hatred."

Yet every group strives to take care of its needy through its particular institutions before appealing to the larger private or public organizations. The Jews, for example, are able to care for all their people. All their organizations raise some money when necessary toward helping their needy families.

The newer groups under the Catholic Church make a valiant, if less successful, attempt. They tend far more than the Protestants to lean heavily upon the parish organizations for support in time of need. The French-Canadian parish is, of course, poorer than the Irish, and finds it more difficult to meet the needs of its members through parish organizations, but its St. Anne's Society, during 1935, spent $950 to aid 130 families, $700 of which was spent for shoes alone, and the St. Vincent de Paul Society spent $1,171.47. In addition, the men's branch of the Saint-Jean-Baptiste Society helped its members during sickness up to the sum of $500 and the women's auxiliary spent $100. The plight of the French-Canadian parish, however, is that no matter how much it would like to be self-sufficient it cannot. Its parishioners are essentially working-class people; those not in need themselves can do only a limited amount to help others. As one mill worker commented: "You help all you can by giving as much money as you can to the church to take care of the needy. After that you just can't worry about it. The town will have to take care of them."

The Irish, through their similar parish organizations, are able to care for those in need much more adequately than are the same organizations in the French-Canadian parish. The St. Anne's Society, for example, spent $3,200 in 1935. This included the distribution of clothes valued up to a thousand dollars, also grocery orders to different stores, and 280 Christmas baskets. The St. Vincent de Paul Society raised $3,000 and aided 200 persons. The Irish point out, however, that most of their aid goes to families of French-Canadian stock who have become members of Cathedral parish.

Altogether, through its parish organizations, the Catholic group raises over eight thousand dollars annually. This money is entirely distributed by volunteer workers to families who might otherwise have to seek aid from the city charity department. Its distribution, however, is not coordinated except in a general sense with the welfare work of the community as a whole, nor is it yet an integrated part of a comprehensive plan among the Catholics. In addition to these parish organizations there are a few societies designed to give service to the general Catholic group, irrespective of the parish to which the needy one may belong. Such organizations usually concentrate on a specific aspect of welfare work; the social service division of the Catholic Daughters of America, for example, is primarily interested in unmarried mothers; the St. Joseph's Orphanage is concerned with looking after children; the Catholic hospital in town and another Catholic hospital a few miles distant care for a number of charity patients.

The Protestants do comparatively little charitable work through organizations primarily identified with their churches. Within all the Protestant churches the money raised for helping those in the parish is a negligible amount, ranging from $52 to about $300 a year. A gesture toward giving Thanksgiving or Christmas baskets to either needy members of the parish or those intimately known to the parish is also made, but actually the Church as an agency through which its members can be helped has largely ceased to function.

Many of the Protestants are a little self-conscious with

regard to the fact that they do so little direct charitable work through their churches, and they explain it in various ways: if members of their own parish are not in need, they cannot very well reach beyond it to help the needy who may be of the Catholic faith; such a gesture would be resented by the Catholics; or, "We don't believe in giving money to people and making them dependent; we aim to help them to help themselves."

At the same time, many of the Old Americans in particular are quick to point out that if they were in need they would rest assured that they would not have to appeal to the town for aid, because the group would never "let them down." But the Old American group has the wealth of the community and few of its members expect to need to appeal for aid. Some of the churches even have to hunt around in order to find a family within the parish to help.

The most important reason for the decline in Protestant church charities is probably to be found in the rise of secular charitable organizations which are more or less exclusively identified with the Protestant group in their control and philosophy. Originally started by public-spirited Old Americans, they still depend for a part of their support upon the Protestant churches. Moreover, it is still customary for their Boards of Directors to be drawn up so that they consist of representatives from each Protestant church. This was done originally, according to an old record book of a local social agency, "because it seemed a natural way of getting charitably minded women to work and of securing the interests of the various churches in giving donations." None of these agencies, however, aim to confine their work exclusively to Protestants, but rather to put their service on a community basis. Today the clientele of every one of them consists very largely of members of the Roman Catholic Church, and especially French Canadians. Nevertheless, because of the nature of their directorships and of their way of handling those in need, they are, in the eyes of the general community, identified with the Protestants.

The difference between the ethnic stock and religious affiliation of the clientele and that of the Boards of Directors and the staffs has presented many problems to the charitable organizations. The natural difficulties the social worker experiences in satisfying both the client's needs and the sponsors' demands have been enhanced by the fact that the two groups differ not only in economic position but also in language and in other important aspects of culture. The importance of these differences is implied in the comment made by French-Canadian clients to a temporary French-Canadian social worker, "Oh, I'm so glad you are French — and a Catholic. I can talk to you."

In an effort to bridge this gap and to gain the fuller coöperation of the newer ethnic groups of the Catholic faith, these social agencies have included among their members either one representative from the Catholic group as such, or one representative from the French-Canadian parish, another from the Irish parish, and a third from the Jewish group. As in a game, this democratic gesture on the part of the Old American Protestant group is met by a "concession" on the part of the Catholic group that its representatives sit on the Boards of Directors of these private social agencies. The results, however, have not always been as successful as was hoped in winning either added financial support or greater coöperation from the Catholic group. The newer board members have occasionally been criticized for their lack of interest or initiative in board meetings. Such criticism seldom takes into account the fact that most of these newer board members have had less social experience than the Old American Protestants, and in addition are not made to feel it their place to make important recommendations to organizations looked upon as essentially American Protestant.

In spite of these difficulties, which time may resolve, the move on the part of these social agencies to make their boards more representative is a significant step forward in bringing about a shared responsibility among the ethnic groups in the community. It has not meant, however, that the boards of these agencies have become really democratic in their basis of selection. So far no effort has been made by the Old American majority on the Boards of Directors to increase the representation from the ethnic groups of the Catholic faith, nor have these boards made any effort to train leaders through appointment of social-minded individuals from the newer groups to committees headed by board members. Instead, these boards usually have chosen to remain, except for their one democratic gesture, more or less inflexible, and frequently self-perpetuating. They may be tired of the responsibility which has been theirs since the inception of many of these organizations, but they are unwilling to yield any of their power to the representatives of the newer ethnic groups of the community who might more closely represent the clientele. Thus, admirable as the work of these agencies frequently is, it cannot be rooted in the widest base of community support.

Thwarted in the hope of gaining the full support of the newer ethnic groups for these agencies, the Old Americans tend to feel that they bear most of the major burden of private charitable activity in the city. They know that their organizations, which are the only ones they are familiar with, serve primarily the Catholic group, and the French Canadians especially, and they feel that the Catholic group gives little financial support. They fail to realize that other organizations, identified with the Catholics in their directorships and technique as well as in their clientele, demand the support of the Catholics, and that these agencies, not including the Catholic hospital, were able to raise $8,321.47 for charitable activity during a depression year from people who were most hard hit by the hard times. It is doubtful whether the Protestants actually give to charity an amount comparable, in view of their proportionately greater ability. Their major charitable organizations raised the following amounts during 1935: The Visiting Nurses, $1,200; the Red Cross, $1,000; the Vermont Children's Aid Society, $3,736.72; the Salvation Army, $5,416.49; and the Mary Fletcher (public) Hospital, $2,541.70. Considering the fact that, though Protestants may have been the largest donors to these organizations, all groups contributed to some extent, there may be some truth to the statement of a finance secretary of a large urban social agency that Burlington does not, according to its population, give to charitable causes the amount that it might give.

It is perhaps because of this lack of wide community support and control that few of the organizations in the community have changed much during their existence. Most of them today are content to stay as they are, trying bravely to meet increasing demands on their time and resources, but trying very seldom to change the basis on which they meet those demands so as to conform perhaps more closely to the changing needs of the community. In even the most progressive agencies there is a conserving attitude, an attempt to maintain policies which are based on interpretations of function which met in the past with the approval of directors, but which today may bear less relation to the changed needs of the community. Perhaps the outstanding example of this trend has been in the Howard Relief Society, organized about 1884 by a wealthy Old American woman. It was the only agency in the city which provided nursing service for the sick, clothed underprivileged children, and aided the poor. At one time it was spoken of as one of the finest private social agencies in any community of this size in New England. Having attained this recognition, all its policies and activities crystallized at that point. For the succeeding twenty-five years it retrogressed until it did little else but provide shoes to the families of needy children in the public schools. After these many years of decline an attempt has been made recently, owing largely to the death of its conservative members, to revive the society and to reorganize it so that it can meet the very great need in Burlington for a family welfare agency.

The organization which, nearer than any other, seems to reflect the entire community, is the Visiting Nurse Association, a semi-public organization which renders health service to all economic and social classes in the community. Organized by a group of Old Americans, it now includes on its board of twenty-seven directors two representatives from the Irish group, two from the French-Canadian, and one from the Jewish. Three of its six nurses are of French-Canadian descent. The Visiting Nurse Association is almost the only community agency which reaches the French-Canadian group settled around the mills in the southern end of the city. By sending there a French-Canadian nurse to teach mothers health measures and to hold baby clinics, it unconsciously does a bigger job of Americanization than any other welfare agency. Yet those of its members who see the wider range of service which this organization could bring to the community know that, with the emphasis on a conservative interpretation of its functions, it will never be able to serve the community in the deeper way which its leaders see as possible.

In addition to these various private organizations which are for the most part identified either with Catholics or Protestants, there is the city Charity Department. Because it is tax-supported, everyone feels that there, at least, he has the right to seek aid. As one French Canadian explained, "We pay our taxes, so the city should help us when we are hard up." Members of practically every ethnic group in the city have appeared on its list, although no more than an occasional Jewish family has availed itself of this community service.

The high expenditure of public money for the care of those in need in recent years has made the Charity Department a target of criticism for political groups with platforms of economy. So far they have not been entirely successful in making the Department a political football, since a requested investigation has revealed the fact that the Department is managed efficiently. It is difficult, however, to prevent whatever political group is in power from insisting that the Charity Department show favoritism to people who have assisted in electing its members to office, and the consequence is that among the poor people themselves there is considerable grievance because some people are getting more than others for no apparent reason. Furthermore, the emphasis on economy, at the expense of effective work, has seriously limited the value of the work which the Department can do. As a result, the general feeling of the community toward the Charity Department is mixed. More or less satisfaction, on the part of those who have not had to use its service, with the idea that the Department is doing a good job with a limited staff is blended with some feeling of irritation at the cost of supporting so many people on the charity list.

Because of this effort to hold down costs, it is inevitable that certain valued social service standards must go by the board. For example, the city fathers, in their understandable desire to be economical, have established a commissary where all those on the charity list must take their weekly grocery order. The value of the commissary is demonstrated by the fact that it has lessened the expenses of the city; what it does in terms of depriving the individual of the feeling of personal responsibility for managing his own life, which is expressed in part by the right to choose his own way of spending money, is apparently considered less important.

This mixture of feeling, this attempt to do good work without spending too much money, is a result of a conflict in the community between the belief that those in need must be helped and the fairly definite conviction that has persisted even during the depression years that "it's pretty much people's own fault if they must ask the city for help, and especially if they must stay on the relief rolls for any length of time." This feeling of resentment on the part of the better established groups within the community is not particularly lessened by the fact that an overwhelming proportion of those on relief are newcomers, Catholics, probably even "foreigners." In 1934, among the families receiving aid only 2 per cent were Protestant, as compared with 98 per cent who were Roman Catholic.

The feeling, moreover, is directed more especially against one particular ethnic group, the French-Canadian, since French-Canadian names appear more frequently on the charity list than those of any other nationality. The public does not always take time to consider that the French Canadians are the largest single ethnic group in the community and comprise by far the largest proportion of that part of the working class which is the most immediately affected by any business depression. Instead, only the large bloc they form on the relief rolls is noted, and this serves to enhance the community attitude toward the French Canadians as social inferiors.

An interesting light is thrown on this situation by the fact that the first-generation French Canadians located in the cotton mill section are proportionately much less "on the town" than are the longer established French Canadians living in the older settled part of the city. The Charity Department has noted that no people have shown any greater thrift, pride, and unwillingness to accept public aid than those first-generation French Canadians at Lakeside. An example is the fact that during the summer of 1934 every family on relief in the cotton mill section of the town had its own garden, whereas of the 615 families receiving relief in Burlington proper only 22 families were willing to assume the work of having gardens. It would seem, then, that at least some of the people of French-Canadian stock who appeal to the city for aid come from either those second- and third-generation families who are in transition between the mores of their own group and the values and standards of living of the American community, or from families who, like some of the Yankee stock, have failed to improve their lot during the last two or three generations and instead have retrogressed. This would seem to indicate that the responsibility rests upon the American community in its economic and social relationships to the children of immigrants as much, at least, as upon the quality of stock of the people.

There is a general recognition that there should be more coöperation among the various social agencies. True, the executives of each agency and society speak highly of the fine coöperative spirit prevailing among the various organizations and of the surprising lack of duplication of effort, but this coöperation is almost wholly of case worker with case worker, or board member with board member; the kind of coöperation that is an agency policy, or that implies a community chest or a council of social agencies or an effective social service exchange does not exist. Recent appeals that all those interested in social work should meet together have encountered enthusiastic response. So far, these meetings have been usually given over to unrelated reports of the work of each agency or to an inspirational talk by one person, but they reflect a reaching out for more coördinated endeavor on the part of all concerned, and may in time lead not only to coördination of effort but to a redefinition of function.

There have been a number of efforts to establish a community chest, but they have not been successful. The Protestant and the Jewish groups feel, with some justification, that such an enterprise would be unsatisfactory without the coöperation of the Catholic agencies; moreover, leading agencies have now been advised that Burlington is too small a city for a successful community chest movement. The city has not so far thought of any alternative way toward a more effective means of raising money for its several charities.

Failing to secure the coöperation implied in the community chest, every agency and organization continues to put on its annual or semi-annual drive for funds independently and there is keen competition for the first call on the community pocketbook. The Vermont Children's Aid Society is the one agency which announces, through the newspapers and through a convention list at the Chamber of Commerce, the date set for its Burlington campaign for funds, whereupon some other organizations, instead of coöperating, seem to vie with each other to get their drives in shortly before the Children's Aid drive begins. Thus during the winter of 1935, just before the Children's Aid Society began its long-planned campaign, the Red Cross, the Boy Scouts, the Y. M. C. A., the Mary Fletcher Hospital, all crowded in their annual drives for funds. As the result of such pressure, each organization fails to get the amount of money hoped for; each campaign drags on interminably. Many organizations, especially the hospitals and the Boy Scouts, make three or more other appeals throughout the year. The newspapers each time roll out an editorial on the worthiness of the cause, but the whole community seems weary and reluctant to respond to the endless requests either to canvass for or to contribute to the financial support of some social agency or organization.

The attempt to establish a social service clearing house

has met with a greater success. None of the fraternal organizations, it is true, make known any of the families to whom they give assistance, but the fact that the Catholic organizations do not coöperate fully is a much more serious matter. Many Catholic organizations and individuals take particular pride in the fact that "we do a lot of charitable work but we don't talk about it." One important step forward has recently been made: during the last two or three years the St. Vincent de Paul Societies and the St. Anne's Societies of the Catholic parishes have taken their lists of clients to check them with the names listed on the rolls of the American Red Cross and the Charity Department; but although the unofficial exchange has been of value to the Catholic agencies, it has been of little assistance to other agencies which, owing to lack of knowledge of the persons being assisted by the Catholic organizations, are unable to ascertain the extent to which duplication of services exists.

In addition to its social service work through agencies and private charities, there are many related social issues which periodically agitate the community. The question of housing, for example, has been revived fitfully ever since a housing survey was made in 1919, but its recommendations in regard to slum areas were not given much publicity when it was discovered that some leading citizens in the community owned some of the shabbiest tenement houses. Social workers have pointed out that few cities have tenement houses comparable in shabbiness to a few of those in which some of Burlington's citizens live. Occasionally the leading citizens are invited to see these, but although the stench at times has made them ill, it is felt that there is nothing that can be done about them. The city health inspector, for instance, does not care to condemn houses as unsanitary nor the fire chief to condemn buildings as not fireproof which are owned by citizens who might be influential in causing these men to lose their positions. Thus one important reform which might result in improving housing conditions for the people concerned is postponed indefinitely.

Recently Burlington has been stirred to realize that from these very shabby tenement areas have come its juvenile delinquents. The Superintendent of the Vermont Industrial School tried to rouse various Burlington organizations and the newspapers to see to it that some action be taken which might lessen the amount of delinquency from three Burlington neighborhoods which produced all of Burlington's delinquents. From one single tenement house, for example, thirty delinquent children have been sent to the state industrial school. If this tendency should continue, the Superintendent pointed out, it would cost Burlington just as much to commit these children to the industrial school as to improve the neighborhood and the social life of its young people. In spite of the brief rousing of interest in this situation, however, the citizens are not moved to attempt to get at the causes of these delinquency areas. The community thought it saw a solution of the problem in the organization of community boys' clubs, but even this effort was thwarted by the failure to secure the coöperation

TENEMENTS IN THE NORTH END

of the head of the Cathedral parish. The priest's only answer to the statement that 80 per cent of these young delinquents were Roman Catholic was that they were not good Catholics; this seemed, at least to him, to absolve him of responsibility in regard to them.

Protestant organizations do not feel that they can go ahead alone in meeting this problem without Catholic coöperation. They remember from previous attempts at organizing boys' clubs, the Boy Scouts in particular, that they have been blocked by the stern Catholic criticism of all such attempts as being primarily proselytizing in nature. So far the two groups have not discovered any way of getting together in the matter. Meanwhile, the Catholic group does not seem to recognize any need for social organizations to care for the leisure time of its poor young people. There is, instead, only a hope that they will stay at home and attend to their school studies and home duties and not get into mischief.

Thus, even in welfare work, community coöperation is difficult to achieve. The economic situation of recent years has only emphasized a lack of coöperation which has long existed. Once again, the very size of the town makes coöperation difficult. It is neither small enough for the churches and an overseer of the poor to meet all needs nor large enough to have such coördination of effort as is implied in a community chest. It cannot accept the impersonal technique of a large city, but it can no longer maintain on a community-wide basis the person-to-person "neighborliness" in charity which it remembers as satisfactory.

Its peoples therefore tend to fall back upon smaller group-ings. Numerous small agencies and societies see their community function in terms of narrow spheres, where they usually render only material aid. Each ethnic and re-ligious group tends to give its first support to those agencies which are indigenous to it and only secondarily supports those agencies identified with social service to the com-munity as a whole. In a simpler community this would not only be adequate, it might also be highly commendable. In a community the size of Burlington it results in the neglect of certain types of problems and in an inadequate and inefficient handling of others. Coöperation of effort in ameliorative activity is essential; the efficiency which such coöperation would permit is a practical necessity; but while increased efficiency is necessary in handling the problems presented, it is not the complete answer, as social workers in many urban centers where such efficiency has been achieved are beginning to understand. The solution called for, many social workers feel, is not only unanimity of approach, but a fresh approach in which charity shall be looked upon not as a more or less unwelcome Christian duty but as a grave social responsibility.

INTERPRETATIONS OF CITIZENSHIP

In their conduct in the civic life of the community, whether in regard to voting, holding public office, or par-ticipating in such civic enterprises as charity, each group plays its part according to its interpretation of citizenship. All, of course, wish to be considered good American citizens, yet in spite of all the effort at standardization in regard to citizenship, interpretations of what it means differ. This was revealed in one way by the spontaneous answers to the question, "Of what nationality do you consider yourself?"

Many persons were quick to respond that this was not a question to ask, that of course we were all Americans, and that the emphasis on differences which such a question implied was detrimental to the endeavor on the part of everyone to set aside his nationality and be American. As one man put it: " 'Nationality groups' has no place in the American scheme of things. It should be banished from the minds of those few who yet consider it a matter of importance. We all came to America for the same purpose, and the mere fact that one family or a group of families saw the light sooner than another should not affect the standing of the others." Yet this very gesture toward ignoring ethnic differences in American life reveals the sensitivity of people in regard to them. True, many considered themselves "American, of course" because they have been identified with America for many generations, but many more, it would seem, answered in that way either because of a blind faith in the American dream of the equality of peoples and classes, or in a defensive manner which reflected a disillusionment in regard to that dream and a wish to believe it true.

Most persons, however, when asked, "Of what nationality do you consider yourself?" named their ethnic stock or gave a hyphenated citizenship. Many considered themselves hyphenated Americans in a really intelligent attempt to give a complete answer; others stated their ethnic stock because of pride of race, especially if it were "Nordic"; still others considered themselves hyphenated citizens not because they wished to emphasize their ethnic origin but because the community as a whole tends to classify people in this manner and they felt that to ignore one's ethnic stock would be comparable to evading the truth about one's age. Thus the answers of many who gave themselves as hyphenated Americans do not necessarily reflect an un-American attitude on their part so much as an un-American attitude of the community as a whole, which persists in so classifying people.

The Old Americans, more than any group, emphasized their ethnic origin or expressed race-consciousness. Sixty-six of the 101 interviewed, when asked their nationality, named their ethnic stock, whether English, Scotch-English, English-Irish, Dutch-English, or other hyphenated-English derivation, and none of these mentioned the fact that they were American also. Twenty-three of the rest called themselves English-Americans, English-Scotch-Americans, and the like; only eleven said simply that they were Americans, and it is significant that a number of these added special qualifications: "I am American, of course. But I don't mean that in the same sense in which the foreigners use it; by American I mean 'pure stock.'" [1] "I am American, of course, but not one of those hundred-percenters that all

---

[1] "Pure stock," when used by an Old American, means English stock.

foreigners try to be." "I consider that we are *the* Americans."

The French Canadians have been noted for their strong consciousness of race and the consequent slowness with which they identify themselves with American civilization, but they were not any more race-conscious than the Old Americans. When asked the question, "Of what nationality do you consider yourself?" 50 per cent of them stated that they were French or French-Canadian; 43 per cent considered themselves Franco-Americans; and 7 per cent called themselves American. This is an unusually high degree of consciousness of race for a people who have been as long established in this country as have a considerable proportion of the French Canadians. It would seem to be due in part to the fact that to many of the first and second generation their nationality is determined by their place of birth or their ethnic stock plus their present citizenship. Thus, many made explanations similar to the following: "My wife is French-Canadian because she was born in Canada and is not naturalized; I am Franco-American because I have become naturalized; my children, born here, are American."

Another factor is the race-consciousness of many of the leaders who are quick to assert their ethnic stock in defense of their people, who, as a whole, because of their place in the economic and social life of the community, have a marked feeling of inferiority. This feeling is manifested by some of the second generation in looking upon all newcomers of their race as foreigners, and by others in denying their own racial stock. The denial of race is seldom successful, however; for whether the individual wishes it or not, he is classed according to his ethnic origin. A French-Canadian woman said to her brother, who wished to consider himself American without the qualification of his ethnic origin: "It is useless to try to deny your nationality and call yourself American — you will give yourself away in one way or another by a gesture or a word. You might as well build up a pride in your nationality and not be ashamed to say what you are. For no matter what you say, people will know you are French-Canadian."

The attitudes toward nationality changed with each generation among the French Canadians. For example, though 87 per cent of the first generation called themselves French Canadians, only 38 per cent of the second and 31 per cent of the third gave this as their nationality. Only a small proportion of the first generation, 10 per cent, called themselves Franco-American; but 51 per cent of the second and 63 per cent of the third classified themselves in this way. Only 3 per cent of the first generation, 11 per cent of the second, and 6 per cent of the third, classified themselves as simply American. That even fewer of the third generation than of the second did so seems to imply that the gesture made by the second generation toward identification with American life has not met with the hoped-for success, and as a result the third generation has been influenced to identify itself to a greater extent with its own ethnic group. This smaller proportion of the third generation who think of themselves as American may be of considerable significance to the future place of the French-Canadian group in the life of the community.

Only three (5 per cent) of the fifty-seven Jews interviewed used any hyphenated term such as Russian-Jews, or even American-Jews; six (11 per cent) considered themselves Americans; the remainder called themselves Jews. Practically all insisted that they were American, but that both community pressure and pride in their religio-cultural heritage make them emphasize the fact that they are Jews. As one young woman explained: "Of course I am American; I know I am American; I was born here. But I don't feel that I am the same as other Americans. If I were applying for a job, it would be expected of me to say that I am Jewish, and I wouldn't care to deceive my employer or anyone else about it; so I always say I am Jewish."

The Irish are very sensitive on the question of nationality. They insist that they are American — Yankees even; that mere priority on the part of the Old Americans doesn't make them any more American than the Irish. At the same time, they wish to emphasize their racial origin. Of the eighty-three Irish interviewed, fifty-eight, or 67 per cent, consider their nationality to be Irish; nine, or 11 per cent, Irish-American; and sixteen, or 22 per cent, American. The change in emphasis in each generation, however, is marked — 90 per cent of the first generation, 63 per cent of the second, and 54 per cent of the third consider themselves Irish; 5 per cent of the first generation, 14 per cent of the second, and 8 per cent of the third, consider themselves Irish-Americans; and 5 per cent of the first, 23 per cent of the second, and 38 per cent of the third, consider themselves Americans. In some contrast to the French Canadians, there is here greater identification of each generation with American life; but that 54 per cent of the third generation should still consider themselves Irish and only 38 per cent consider themselves American is worthy of note.

Sensitivity to the American reaction against the Hitler regime may have influenced the Germans in their answers to the question "Of what nationality do you consider yourself?" They have recognized, since the rule of Hitler, a revival of the prejudice which developed against them during the World War, and they were therefore extremely cautious in answering. This is undoubtedly part of the reason why a larger proportion of the Germans than of any other group emphasized the fact that they were American; 41 per cent, or fourteen of the thirty-four interviewed, gave their nationality thus, while an equal number described themselves as German; and six, or 18 per cent, as German-American.

Many of the Italians, like the French Canadians, consider that nationality is determined by place of birth, irrespective of whether one is a naturalized citizen of another country or not. Twenty-eight, or 70 per cent, of the forty Italians interviewed said they were Italians, four that they were Italian-Americans, and the other eight that they were Americans. That such a large proportion of the Italians, who are mostly members of the first generation in America, should call themselves American reflects the great desire on the part of this group to be identified with American life. At the same time, it reflects, too, that the faith in America as a land where class distinctions are dissipated, where equal opportunity rests for all, is an ideal that is cherished most among the newest peoples of the country.

Although every group in one way or another expressed its identification with American life in its insistence that it was American, yet the statements also made it clear that the ethnic traditions which color the interpretation of citizenship cannot be ignored. All the gestures toward standardizing one-hundred-per-cent Americanism are futile against the weight of cultural traditions of generations. Somehow or other every group felt that the two forces of loyalty to America and loyalty to their cultural heritage should be merged. This was revealed in part when members of each group were asked whether they agreed, disagreed, or were uncertain in regard to the following statement: "Each nationality group in America should maintain something of its own identity." Eighty-three per cent agreed with the statement, 4 per cent were uncertain, and 13 per cent disagreed. The French-Canadian, Jewish, and Irish groups, respectively, were more emphatic than the others in their affirmation — 97 per cent of the French Canadians, 89 per cent of the Jews, and 82 per cent of the Irish taking an affirmative stand. Nor was there any change in attitude in these groups between the first, second, and third generations.

In preserving something of its own culture, each group was most concerned with the element of language. Attitude scales in regard to the preservation of language revealed that even the Old Americans and the Irish considered it worth while for the non-English-speaking groups to preserve their own languages to some extent, provided it did not stand in the way of knowing English at least equally well. The Germans expressed a similar attitude. Yet opinions varied among these three English-speaking groups. One point of view was expressed in such remarks as the following: — "I think that national groups should become in every way Americanized. This means speaking the language first of all." "To make a solid nation you must have one language, otherwise there will be no solidarity of ideas." A divergent point of view was expressed in such remarks as: — "If I were in another country I should want my children to have English. Therefore I concede to the newcomers to this country their right to the language." "I believe in all cultural additions to life, of which language is one. I do not think that keeping the mother tongue need interfere with loyalty to the United States."

The three groups which put greatest emphasis on preserving their language are the Italian, Jewish, and French-Canadian, but the Italians have little more than a hope that their language may be preserved in their homes. None of them feel that Italian should be spoken in preference to English; more than half of them consider that mostly English should be spoken. As one of their leading citizens explained, "We should know Italian because it is our language, but we should all know English better, because we live in America. We will progress faster if we all speak English." The attitude of the Jews toward preserving their language differed from that of other groups; the second generation expressed little interest in its preservation, not considering it as important in promoting the cohesion of the group as do the French Canadians. As one man explained it: "One can preserve the Jewish culture without Yiddish. That isn't the mother tongue anyway. Preserve Hebrew, however, because persecution will require it." Concerning the future of the Yiddish language there are two opposing points of view: one based on faith in the ultimate assimilation of all peoples; the other on the fear that at some time the Jews may be reminded of their separateness. One point of view was expressed as follows: "With our system of public education, and with the Jew's desire to take advantage of every opportunity to better himself, which he can do only by contact with the majority group; with immigration discouraged, thereby shutting off the Jewish group, the disappearance of the Yiddish language is inevitable." In contradistinction to this is the comment: "There is always a renaissance among the Jewish people, usually brought about through persecution. Good times make you forget the language, and on the surface it would seem that Yiddish will disappear, but history proves otherwise."

More than any group, the French Canadians emphasize preserving their language. Self-conscious as they may be about the French-Canadian *patois,* they know that the French language will live as the recognized language of culture for even the English-speaking world. Consequently, the third generation was as positive as were the first and the second in regard to the desirability of preserving their language. As one woman explained: "Why shouldn't we keep our language? It is the most beautiful language. The Yankees send their children to college to learn it."

Thus every ethnic group took the stand that something of its language and its culture should be preserved. This, they were convinced, was in no way incompatible with the finest loyalty to America. When, however, each individual was asked, "What do you consider constitutes being a good American citizen?" many found it difficult to answer. Some considered that it was too serious a question to be answered in any one interview; others seemed to have too vague a concept of citizenship to be able to express it in any way. Those who did answer usually defined their attitudes in terms of the nationalistic slogans which we have been brought up to accept. They did not give evidence of any profound consideration of fundamental attributes of citizenship, but all listed the qualifications for being a good citizen in the following order: respecting and obeying the laws, upholding the Constitution, being loyal and patriotic, defending the country, respecting public institutions, living up to American traditions.

The variation between the groups, however, in the emphasis put upon certain attributes, was interesting in reflecting characteristic differences in attitudes. A comment frequently made by Old Americans was, "A good American is one who gives more to the country than he takes from it." The Irish often explained: "Belong to the church; when faithful to that, you will live up to everything that follows."

The French Canadians and the Italians emphasized *knowing* and respecting the laws — a reflection of the fact that they do not feel as much at home in this country as some other groups; paying taxes, voting, then living up to American traditions. Along with these standard attributes of good citizenship, these groups put emphasis on quality of character, perhaps implied in the answers given by the other groups. Their remarks frequently were as follows: "Obey the Ten Commandments; then one would be a perfect American." "Don't play with money, don't quarrel, support your family — makes you a good citizen." "Try to become American and plan to stay here, not to go back to the Old Country after earning some money." The French Canadians in particular emphasized, "Being peaceful with all other nationalities here is most important." Incidentally, no other group made this comment.

It may be true that there is not much to be expected in any spontaneous response to a question with as many implications as has the question: "What do you consider constitutes being a good American citizen?" The real feeling that people have toward their responsibilities is possibly much more profound than the answers they give. Nevertheless, their statements reveal what is on the top of their minds when they consider citizenship. It also reflects the extent to which they have let automatic reactions relieve them of the necessity of considering their obligations. Being an American citizen is something into which most of us have been born, as we have been born into the Republican party or the Christian Church. What these affiliations mean we seldom stop to consider. The various slogans which we use to avoid such consideration reveal the possibility of developing a narrow nationalism which may kill the very meaning of liberty implied in some of the slogans. They reveal that the common denominator of our interpretation of American citizenship is not at a very high level. Certainly in none of the answers given was there any recognition of the creative responsibilities of citizenship as interpreted by H. A. Overstreet in *We Move in New Directions*:

When, then, is one patriotic in the genuine sense of this word? The answer is: when one defends or advances the contributory powers of one's country. This will require something quite different from a readiness to defend with musket or poison gas. It will require a willingness to be alert to all the forces that threaten the contributory powers that struggle to expression in one's midst. Thus it will be patriotic to oppose the stirrers-up of mass passion against other people; it will be patriotic to take action against those who, in novel or play or film or newspaper, arouse prejudice by flagrant misrepresentations; it will be patriotic to work against those in one's own land or elsewhere who exploit the lives of the defenseless for their own selfish purposes. There will, in short, be the obligation to defend life-values against those who seek to destroy them. But it will be patriotic, too, to make disinterested research in laboratories, to invent, to write books, to compose music, to organize wholesome recreation.

Genuine patriotism, in short, will consist in all those attitudes and activities that defend and support universally shareable values.

From this point of view, the patriotism that can hound a Kreisler during wartime, or cast out the language and literature of a great people from the schools and colleges because that language and literature happen to belong to the enemy, has its place on a sub-civilized level of life. In future, many more of us may be willing to go to prison rather than have commerce with that species of pernicious provincialism. Contributory patriotism is cast in more generous mold. It is a loyalty to those great shareable values that both support and overarch the processes and groupings of our life and that give us the only justification for regarding the human race as of any significance whatever. It was of such loyalty that Euripides was doubtless thinking when he wrote: "Every land is fatherland to noble men." [1]

[1] New York: W. W. Norton and Company, Inc., 1933, pp. 207–208.

CHAPTER XI

THE WAY AHEAD

W E HAVE seen in what fashion the various peoples of Burlington live together and work out their problems in an area of common endeavor. All are motivated by the basic forces and pervasive ideals of our society, not the least of which is the compulsion to conformity. This emphasis on conformity is understandable in a country such as ours which alone has had to cope from the very beginning of its history with the problem of molding into a unified people an overwhelming number of representatives of all the diverse elements of the earth. Outwardly, in appearance, manners, and certain habits, all these peoples have succeeded in fitting into one mold, but beneath the common surface there remain differences that have refused to yield to the process of the melting pot.

The casual observer can see that the differences among the peoples of any community are cultural as well as biological. Some ethnic groups are represented largely by persons whose forebears have been peasants for many centuries, others are represented more largely by persons identified with middle-class business and the professions. Some show marked aptitudes in government, others in art or industry. The level of achievement as well as the rate of advance has differed from group to group. Yet, oblivious to the forces which determine each individual's contribution to America, we have chosen to ignore these very differences in our great effort to see a standardized American, whose value to society shall be measured by the extent to which he conforms to a common pattern, either advances himself materially or desires to do so, and is willing therefore to accept the standards of those who have.

For this reason the potentialities of our diverse population have remained very largely unrealized. Differences which might have been contributory to a general community have been permitted to become bases for distinction in themselves, or to enhance the economic and social stratification that tends to develop in any established society. The failure to see through our religious and racial prejudices and preferences and to build up a standard, comprehensive of differences, by which individual worth might more justly be evaluated, attests the short distance we have moved from primitive society and its characteristics. The inability to appreciate fully the values of other peoples, when it occurs in primitive societies, is called ethnocentrism. It has been described as follows:

Ethnocentrism is the technical name for this view of things in which one's own group is the center of everything, and all others are scaled and rated with reference to it. . . . Each group nourishes its own pride and vanity, boasts itself superior, exalts its own divinities, and looks with contempt on outsiders. Each group thinks its own folkways the only right ones, and if it observes that other groups have other folkways, these excite its scorn. . . . Ethnocentrism leads a people to exaggerate and intensify everything in their own folkways which is peculiar and which differentiates them from others.[1]

---

[1] William Graham Sumner, *Folkways* (Boston: Ginn and Company, 1907), p. 13.

As applied to our modern society, this characteristic has been interpreted in the following manner:

> Ethnocentrism, then, is essentially narrowness. It is enthusiasm for our own due to ignorance of others. It is an appreciation of what we have and a depreciation of what differs. It is essentially a lacking of sympathetic dramatization of the point of view of another.[1]

In a more general sense, such narrowness is not peculiar to the ethnic group. It is to be found in any form of sectionalism. It is aggressive on the part of some people, defensive on the part of others. In either case it precludes a recognition of common elements and common goals. At the present time it most frequently takes the form of seeing the welfare of the country in terms of the particular needs and desires of one's own group — old-age pensions, American Legion patriotism, protection of the small business man or of the big business man. In Burlington, however, ethnocentrism is written less in such terms than in religious terms, Catholic versus Protestant.

In its purely religious aspect, ethnocentrism in Burlington makes it difficult for either the Catholics or the Protestants to find the things they share in common. Each group is represented by a considerable number of people who believe that theirs is the only true religion and that the other is folly. Neither group will look over the walls of its prejudice long enough to discover their basic unity of

[1] Ellsworth Faris, "The Nature of Human Nature," in *The Urban Community* edited by Ernest W. Burgess (Chicago: University of Chicago Press, 1926), p. 28.

approach, except perhaps as they find common ground in a pervasive prejudice against such an outsider as the Jew. This religious cleavage, however, is only in part based on religious differences as such. Under its banner other differences seek expression. The differences of social class, of economic status, tend to be enhanced by the fact that they form along the older religious divisions. True, there are counteracting forces: throughout America Catholics and Protestants are to be found at every level of economic and social life; in a community such as Burlington, individuals behind the Catholic and Protestant fronts are discovering like interests, usually those of class. These have not yet to any great extent become common interests, but the extent to which they tend to do so is a measure of the extent to which class divisions may be superseding religious distinctions.

Behind the major cleavage, looked upon as religious, is also the struggle of each ethnic group to maintain or to achieve a place in the sun. This may not be part of the daily concern of every individual of each group, but every little while the groups take count to see wherein one or the other holds leadership. The Old Americans, though they may be tired of some of the responsibilities which accompany the satisfaction of holding power, are yet loath to yield their place, privilege, or prerogatives to the newer elements. The leadership of the latter group is personified in the Irish, who see themselves as the logical successors to the Old Americans. Behind the Irish, enlisted primarily on a religious basis, are massed the largest element in

Burlington's population, the French Canadians. They may yield unwillingly to the Irish, since, it is generally felt, they distrust them more than they do the Old Americans; but since the Irish, as well as being Catholics, are leaders in the party that has come to be looked upon as the working men's party, the French Canadians tend more and more to accept Irish leadership politically.

Taking no dominant part in this struggle are the Jews. By subtle distinctions and discriminations they frequently are reminded that they are not part of the community in the same way that other groups are. When the anti-Semitic Silver Shirts can be organized in Burlington, when even the nursery school in the community refuses admission to a child solely because she is Jewish, the Jew is made to realize what a powerful self-perpetuating force is the prejudice against him.

Burlington realizes that ethnic and religious factors play an important role in the life of the community. But when individuals were asked, "Can you suggest practical steps by which greater coöperation can be brought about among the different groups in Burlington?" the answer was usually a shake of the head, and the remark: "It's a tough proposition. I'm afraid you can't do anything about it." A large number decided that it wasn't worth doing anything about, that the situation was as satisfactory as could be expected. Time would resolve this matter of ethnic and religious differences, and meanwhile coöperation exists to the extent to which all members of the community actually want it. Some, however, were more concerned with the lack of coöperation, and made various suggestions for broader community spirit and coöperative enterprise.

One such suggestion was that Catholics and Protestants sit down together in an informal way to discuss their differences in the hope that some of these differences might thereby be more clearly understood. Some formal effort to achieve this kind of coöperation has taken place: an attempt has been made to organize a local branch of the National Conference of Jews and Christians; but the problem of getting a Protestant, a Jew, and a Catholic to sit down together to discuss their interpretation of community and in what respects they can coöperate is difficult to achieve. There is a feeling that the church, since one of its main functions is to spread the gospel of brotherly love, should assume greater responsibility in achieving coöperation in Burlington, but a formal expression of it on Brotherhood Day, for example, has only gone as far as to have each congregation pray in its separate church for greater brotherly love among Protestants, Catholics, and Jews. A few persons pointed out that some adult Sunday School classes are interested in the question of furthering better understanding of the black and yellow races, but that the less dramatic task of achieving a richer relationship between different peoples in the community is not touched. Neither Catholic, Protestant, nor Jewish group has tried to bring young people from the various groups together in the same room to learn about each other's religious beliefs. Indoctrination in religion is still too important a factor in our culture to permit the freedom of religious thought that this measure would imply.

Many Burlingtonians put their faith in the public school as the chief agency for lessening racial and religious prejudices and for cultivating racial and religious appreciation; suggestions were made that supervised play and drama could be lessons in ethnic and religious appreciation. Others, however, pointed out that such a solution places too much reliance on one institution to outweigh all the other influences in the daily life of the child, and furthermore, that all the children are not in one public school system.

Among those who placed their faith in the public schools, many felt that the various clubs could continue where the schools left off in education toward finer understanding. They suggested that the Catholic, Protestant, and Jewish women's clubs, in particular, might coördinate their programs more frequently, for the impression prevails in the community that it is the women who preserve prejudicial attitudes to a greater extent than the men. Many members of the Lions Club, for example, pointed out that in their club an unusually democratic spirit prevails among all the members until the day when they invite their wives to attend a meeting; then all the complexities of social distinction stand out in high relief.

Suggestions are occasionally brought up that the schools in each neighborhood should be used in the evenings for adult classes. So far, however, the community finds it difficult to conceive of reaching out this way, preferring to depend upon the people to come to such night school classes as are offered in the public high school, in the center of town. A group of Baptist women have been giving individual instruction in English at home to foreign women who desired it, coupled with an exchange of ideas concerning customs and manners, but this is the only gesture toward a more intimate personal relationship between any members of the newer and the older elements.

The foregoing were the major suggestions given by the few Burlingtonians actively interested in furthering greater coöperative endeavor and appreciation in the community. To these, the pursuit of such steps could be the first important gestures out of which greater coöperation might be developed. To others, however, they ring a little hollow and seem to look too much to understanding and tolerance as solutions in themselves. As Rabbi Jacob J. Weinstein pointed out:

> Tolerance is not enough. We must make America not only safe for differences but actively appreciative of them. When so many of our fellow-Americans still want for bread and shelter, when there are slums to clean and diseases to conquer, when we must still grapple honestly with the criminal paradox of our age — poverty in the midst of plenty — it is a little irrelevant, and more than a little foolish, is it not, for Jews to quarrel with Christians over ancient dogmas, or white to hate blacks, or Protestants to dislike Catholics? Black reaction, fascism, war, the evil furies of our day, threaten our whole civilization. Only a cooperative humanity can successfully meet their ominous challenge.[1]

---

[1] Radio Address of Rabbi Jacob J. Weinstein, of the Editorial Staff of *Opinion*, WEVD, New York. Quoted from *New Relationships with Jews and Catholics* (New York: Association Press, 1934), pp. 59–60.

Yet if any steps in this direction are to be taken, a re-orientation of purpose is necessary, growing out of an understanding of the forces, both in the general culture of our times and in Burlington's particular way of life, which dictate the present situation and influence the future possibilities.

The city of Burlington represents a transitional phase in American life. It lies, historically, somewhere between the rural culture of our past and the developing urban industrial culture of our present and future. The philosophy of its business men is still mainly that of the rugged individualism of farmers in surrounding towns. Lacking any big industries, it lags behind in the social attitudes and concerns of industrial centers. Yet it is in reality sufficiently a part of the modern world so that, though it may look at its problems from an older point of view, the problems it looks at are the same as those of newer industrial centers. Beneath the cleavage between Catholic and Protestant of which the community is aware is the larger social struggle faced by the country as a whole, and the direction which this struggle is taking must be understood if such communities as Burlington are to work out their problems in line with progressive rather than retrogressive development.

Certainly Burlington has a heritage to be highly valued in time of social change. The integrity, independence, and sense of personal control of one's destiny which developed out of an earlier and rural America have been among the virtues most cherished in our culture. These are qualities still to be found in the transitional way of life which is Burlington's. There also exists in that community the sense of security to be derived from the intimacy of a small group. The very existence of strongly self-conscious French-Canadian, Irish, Jewish, and Old American groups gives to the individual the person-to-person support which is an essential basis for his development; each individual can feel he is somebody, at least to a small group if not to the community as a whole. Most people who have seen the breakdown of such small units in our larger urban centers, and have observed the consequent disorganization of human beings offered nothing to replace the security of which they have been deprived, find in Burlington's way of life values we can ill afford to lose.

On the other hand, it must be remembered that we pay full price for the virtues our culture develops at any period. The admired independence of character of rural America may not be valuable in the same way in an interdependent civilization. The sense of security that the small group gives may prove so coercive a force for conformity that spontaneous and expansive life is smothered and creative activity blocked. In the face, therefore, of the social reorganization that is taking place in America, the task ahead of such communities as Burlington is not to worship their virtues as absolutes but realistically to adapt them to the complex demands of a changing world.

The dangers that may arise from an undue emphasis on conserving, instead of developing, must be recognized. Honoring certain values, we tend to believe that the institutions which expressed those values at a particular stage of development must remain unchanged. Fearing un-Americanism, the community may yield its very independence of thought and freedom to some narrow concept of Americanism. Then the very ethnic and religious prejudices which still live in the community may be forged into the tools by which a demagogue can further divide the population and stultify human development.

To avoid these dangers, such communities as Burlington must face the fact that they are inextricably a part of our modern industrial world. They cannot withdraw from its influence. They must therefore make the personal values of their established way of life the other side of the more impersonal coöperative relationships of new and expanding units. Only this will permit the development essential to a democracy. Only in this direction can the very individualism which is so important to such communities express the rich possibilities within it that have never yet been tapped. Only by moving in such a direction can America be the reality as well as the symbol of the land of the free.

APPENDICES

APPENDIX A

METHODS USED

The material for this study was gathered in many different ways. Informal discussion with leaders of the several ethnic groups in the community first brought out the nature of the problem of ethnic adjustment as it presented itself in Burlington. Perhaps the most valuable information in regard to the life of the city was obtained in this manner, without any set schedule or questionnaire. These informal discussions not only continued throughout the study, but were used as a base in laying out the detailed questionnaire later followed.

After the general nature of the problem in Burlington was ascertained, a census of the householders of the city was made during the summer of 1933; 4,477 householders were at home when this canvass was made, and their information supplied basic data as to the place of birth and nationality of each, and, if married, of his wife; place of birth of the parents of each; length of residence in the United States; size of family for selected ethnic groups; and the names and city addresses of adult children who were third-generation Americans. A spot map was made of the ethnic character of the city, and statistics were compiled of all suitable data.

With the information thus gathered as a base, detailed questionnaires such as that given in Appendix B were drawn up in order to obtain general information and ascertain social attitudes in the community. From the card index made during the preliminary survey according to nationality of the householder, 459 persons were selected for detailed interview, being chosen so as to obtain a representative number of each of six ethnic groups and of the generations within each group. They were also chosen to supply as fair a sampling as possible of working-class and business-class persons. Since most of the interviews took place during the daytime, a large proportion of them were with women; care was taken, therefore, to choose, except for a few instances in each group, women whose ethnic stock was the same as that of their husbands. The persons to be interviewed were also selected so as to have a fair sampling from every part of the city, but the greatest proportion of those chosen for detailed interview were from those sections of the city in which each ethnic group had the largest representation.

These interviews were distributed among the various ethnic groups as follows: 101 interviews were made among the Old American or Yankee group; 144 were made among the French Canadians; 83 among the Irish; 57 among the Jews; 40 among the Italians; and 34 among the Germans. Other ethnic groups, such as the Greeks and Syrians, were so small that they were not touched in the detailed interviews. Some information was gathered about each of these groups, however, by informal discussions with certain members. Each interview lasted from two to three hours. Of the total number made, 335 were with women and 124 with men. Among the Old American group, 66 were interviews with women and 35 with men; among the Irish, 59 were with women and 24 with men; among the French Canadians, 126 with women and 18 with men; among the Jews, 35 with women and 22 with men; among the Italians, 29 with women and 11 with men; among the Germans, 20 with women and 14 with men.

The author was assisted in making these interviews by the secretary of the Eugenics Survey and by six women, each representing a different ethnic group. These women were supplied by the Vermont Emergency Relief Association and were in the main well qualified for their task. All of them either were college graduates or had had experience in teaching or in business. All were long-established members of the community and each was well identified with her particular ethnic group. Because of this identification they were able to obtain much valuable cultural information. In an effort to supplement the small number of interviews among the Germans and among the men of the French-Canadian group, the author had a number of informal talks with the Germans, and with the French Canadians at their work or in the evenings.

Additional information was obtained from historical gazetteers, city reports, records and programs of clubs and societies, and newspapers. Questionnaires were sent to clubs, lodges, and other social organizations in regard both to their programs and to the representation of the various ethnic groups in their membership. Since the city has a population of less than 25,000, the Census material was unavailable, so that information concerning occupations had to be secured largely from the City Directory.

APPENDIX B

QUESTIONNAIRE USED IN INTERVIEWING THE FRENCH CANADIANS

(In interviewing a German, Italian, or Irishman, the name of his group was used wherever in this sample questionnaire the name "French Canadian" occurs.)

1. Name .... Address .... Ages: Husband .... Wife ....
2. Birthplace:
   Husband .... Father .... Mother .... Nationality .... Generation ....
   Wife .... Father .... Mother .... Nationality .... Generation ....
3. Of what nationality do you consider yourself? .... Naturalized? ....
4. Years in U. S. .... In Burlington ....
   Home: Owned .... Rented ....
5. Why did your people come to the United States? ....
6. Do you ever go back to the old country for a visit? ....
7. Would you care to live there now? .... Why? ....
8. Occupation:
   Husband ... In the old country? ... Father ... In the old country? ..
   Wife ... In the old country? ... Father ... In the old country? ...
   What seems to be the future for your husband in his work? ....
9. Church: How often do you attend church per month? ....
   Which church do you like best, St. Joseph's or Cathedral? .... Why? ....
10. Clubs, Societies, and Organizations:

	Name	Nature	People
Husband:	......	......	......
Wife:	......	......	......
Children:	......	......	......

11. What do you do in your spare time?
    Read .... Cards .... Movies .... Dances .... Visit .... Clubs ....
    Church Affairs ....
    Which of these do you and your husband do together? ....
12. Of what nationality are most of your friends? ....
    Do you come in contact with any American Protestants? ....
    Under what circumstances? Boss .... Business .... Civic ....
    Neighborhood .... At Home ....
13. Education: Husband .... Wife .... Children: Total .... Living ....
    Grades Completed

14. How far do you plan to send your children in school?
    Have you any plans for what you would like your children to do?
    What do your children say they would like to be?

15. What language do you speak at home? .... Read English? .... Read French? ....Can your children understand French? Speak it? Read it? Why?

16. Do you take any French newspapers or magazines?
    What other papers do you take?
    Do you ever get books from the public library?
    Often .... Occasionally .... Never ....

17. Have you a radio? Do you listen in to French-Canadian programs?

18. Do you usually vote? .... Always .... Occasionally .... Never ....
    Are you a Republican or a Democrat? .... How did you decide to which party to belong? ....

19. What difficulties, if any, has your nationality made for you in feeling at home in an Old American community? ....

20. What difficulties, if any, were there for your parents because of their nationality in feeling at home in this Old American community? ....

21. What are the chief difficulties for you as a French Canadian in bringing up your children in this Old American community? *i.e.,* language, customs, obeying?

22. How does the feeling that you have about your nationality differ from
    (a) The feeling your parents had about it? ....
    (b) The feeling your children have about it? ....

23. Have you or any of your friends, because of your nationality or race

(a) Ever found it hard to get a job or make advancement in it?	(b) Known of prejudice being shown to people of your nationality when it comes to running for public or political office?	(c) Have you ever been shown any slights socially or been made to feel self-conscious because of your nationality by any other nationality group?
Yes or no	....	....
Instance	....	....

24. Did your parents experience any such prejudices? ....

25. If so, do you think that this prejudice has lessened or increased? ....

26. How do you account for this change? ....

27. By people of what nationalities have you felt these discriminations most keenly? ....

28. What do you consider are the chief characteristics and contributions of the following nationalities to Burlington?

French Canadians ....   Germans ....
Irish ....   Italians ....
Yankees ....   Syrians ....
Jews ....   Greeks ....

29. If you were perfectly free to choose your neighbors from among these nationalities, in what order would you list your preferences? ....

30. Do you consider this statement right?
    (1) People of French-Canadian descent should speak only French, subscribe only to French newspapers, read only French books, and not use the English language.

31. Does one of the following statements more nearly express your attitude?
    (2) French Canadians should speak mostly French, subscribe mostly to French newspapers, read mostly French books, but learn English for business purposes.
    (3) French Canadians should speak French in their homes, subscribe to French and American newspapers, read both French and American books, and speak English in their business and daily contacts.
    (4) French Canadians should speak mostly English, subscribe mostly to American newspapers, read mostly American books, but should retain some French in the house for value in preserving French culture and traditions.
    (5) French Canadians should drop their language entirely, speak only English, subscribe only to American newspapers, read only American books.

32. If you would preserve the French language, how would you go about doing so? ....
    Do you think this would be effective? ....

33. Do you think the French language will eventually disappear in the United States? ....

34. Do you think other nationalities should retain their language in the United States? ....

35. If the people of each of the nationalities were to keep their language and customs, do you think they would be just as good Americans? ....

36. What do you consider constitutes being a good American? ....

37. Do you consider this statement correct?
    (1) People of French-Canadian descent should live in one section of the city, maintain a distinct French-Canadian culture and community life, and not participate in the interests and activities of the city as a whole.

38. Does one of the following statements more nearly express your attitude?
    (2) Most of the French Canadians should live in one section of the city, centering their interests and activities almost entirely in the

French-Canadian community life, but participate to some extent in the civic and social affairs of the city as a whole.

(3) Half the French Canadians should live in one section of the city, so that a distinct French-Canadian culture and community life might be maintained, but all should participate as much in the interests and activities of the city as a whole as in the French-Canadian community life.

(4) Only a very small portion of the French Canadians should live in one section of the city, so that a very little of the French-Canadian culture and community life might be preserved; but all should participate much more in the general activities and interests of the city as a whole than in the French-Canadian community life.

(5) French Canadians should scatter about the city, make no effort to preserve their language, customs, and community life, and become absorbed into the general American community.

39. Do you think the same should apply to other nationality groups in Burlington, for example, the Jews, Italians, Irish? ....

40. Do you consider this statement correct?
    (1) People of French-Canadian descent should marry only French Canadians.

41. Does one of the following statements more nearly express your attitude?
    (2) People of French-Canadian descent should marry only French Canadians, Frenchmen, or people of similar racial origin and religion?
    (3) People of French-Canadian descent should be free to marry any white American or French Canadian. .... Same religion?
    (4) People of French-Canadian descent should be free to marry anyone within the white race..... Same religion? ....
    (5) People of French Canadian descent should be free to marry anyone of any race or creed.

42. To what extent do you think the same should apply to other nationalities, *e.g.*, Irish, Italians, Jews? ....

43. What to your knowledge have been the outstanding difficulties of intermarriage?
    (a) With persons of different nationality but same religion? ....
    (b) With persons of different nationality and different religion? ....

44. Do you consider this statement correct?
    (1) Children of French-Canadian descent should receive their entire education — elementary. high school, and college — in parochial schools.

45. Does one of the following statements more nearly express your attitude?
    (2) Children of French-Canadian descent should receive their elementary and high school education in parochial schools, but if they

continue their education after that, should attend a public college or university.

(3) Children of French-Canadian descent should receive their elementary education in the parochial schools but continue their high school and college education in public schools.

(4) Children of French-Canadian descent should receive their entire education within the public school system for the most part, so long as they attend parochial schools long enough to learn the Catechism.

(5) Children of French-Canadian descent should receive their entire education — elementary, high school, and college — in the public schools.

46. If your children go to parochial school, do they meet public school children who are (a) of older American or Yankee stock and Protestant? . . . . (b) Jewish? . . . .

47. Through what agencies do they meet? . . . .

48. To what extent do you want your children to mingle with
  (a) Children of other nationalities but same religion . . . .
  (b) Children of other nationalities and of different religion:
    Protestant . . . .
    Jewish . . . .

49. Would you be interested in encouraging more ways by which the young people of all nationalities in the community might get together? . . . .

50. Why? . . . .

51. What French-Canadian customs that your mother kept do you no longer keep, at least to the same extent? (e.g., those connected with birth, courtship, marriage, baptism, death). . . . .

52. What American customs have you adopted that your mother did not keep? (e.g., exchanging Christmas gifts . . . . Christmas cards . . . . Thanksgiving . . . . Honeymoon . . . .)

53. To what extent do you agree to the following statements? (Agree, uncertain, disagree.)

(1) Children should be taught more history of their own nationality in school.

(2) Social disturbances in other nations affect our attitude toward the people of that nationality in our own community.

(3) Each nationality group should take care of its own needy.

(4) The government's assuming responsibility for the care of the unemployed and needy is a great step forward in social progress.

(5) When two men, both well qualified, are running for public office in our city, one should vote for the man who is a member of one's own nationality.

(6) Spiritual reward in the future life determines the extent to which one assumes responsibility about social problems here.

(7) Every nationality group in America should preserve something of its own identity.

(8) Intermarriage will eventually cause all the nationality groups in America to disappear.

(9) One is criticized by the people of one's own nationality if one mixes freely with people of other nationalities.

(10) In deciding the extent to which one should work with people of other religious faiths in social and civic activities in the city, one should be governed by the advice of the church.

(11) Religious difference is the greatest barrier in preventing people from working together harmoniously in this community.

(12) Difference in nationality is a barrier preventing people from working together harmoniously in this community.

54. Do you think that the different nationality groups in Burlington intermingle in the civic and social life of the community? .... Should they intermingle more? ....
Why? ....

55. What do you think are the greatest obstacles in the way of greater coöperation and intermingling among the different nationality groups of Burlington? ....

56. What agencies in our city are most effective in bringing people of different nationalities together? (e.g., Schools .... School games .... Parent-Teacher Associations .... Mothers' Clubs .... Charity Work .... Scouts .... Elks .... Bridge Clubs .... Other ....).

57. Can you suggest any practical steps by means of which greater coöperation and intermingling of the different national groups in Burlington might be brought about?

INDEX

INDEX